Ca... ...Denis Thatcher and Baroness Thatcher, the former Prime Minister. She is a journalist, broadcaster, and author of *Below the Parapet: the Biography of Denis Thatcher*, *Lloyd on Lloyd* and *Diary of an Election*. She lives in London.

CAROL THATCHER

MY STORY

A SWIM-ON PART IN THE GOLDFISH BOWL

headline
review

First published in 2008
by HEADLINE REVIEW
An imprint of Headline Publishing Group

First published in paperback in 2009
by HEADLINE REVIEW

1

Cataloguing in Publication Data is available from the British Library

ISBN 978 0 7553 1708 0

Typeset in Goudy Old Style by Avon DataSet Ltd,
Bidford-on-Avon, Warwickshire

Printed in the UK by CPI Mackays, Chatham, ME5 8TD

HEADLINE PUBLISHING GROUP
An Hachette UK Company
338 Euston Road
London NW1 3BH

www.headline.co.uk
www.hachette.co.uk

CONTENTS

Chapter One

INTRODUCTION

CAUTIOUSLY OPTIMISTIC. THAT'S how I felt as I waited to see who would be crowned Jungle Queen and winner of ITV's 2005, *I'm a Celebrity . . . Get Me Out of Here* programme. Would it be me, or would it be the beautiful, charismatic actress Sheree Murphy of *Emmerdale* soap fame?

'Cautiously optimistic' was a phrase often used by my mother during elections, in the anxious hours between the end of polling and the moment the results were known. I also felt as she had when, shortly before the 1983 general election, an interviewer asked her if she was nervous. 'No,' she said, 'I'm not nervous. I'll just take whatever comes now. We've done our best, and a bit more.'

But *I'm a Celebrity* wasn't about my mother – although there had been plenty of references to her during my stay in Australia's rainforest. The viewers had voted the other ten contestants out, one by one, and now only Sheree and I were left. This was about us – about me. After all the years of being referred to – in fact, virtually defined – as 'the prime minister's daughter', 'Maggie's daughter', 'Mark Thatcher's sister' and so on, during my seventeen-day jungle adventure, people had at last seen me as myself, doing something of my own choice.

While we awaited the public's verdict, it occurred to me that my vicarious political upbringing was going to be very useful training for this nerve-racking countdown to the end of a reality TV show. Sheree and I sat down on one of the logs that bordered the fire, the heart of the camp, and took a last look around. This modest-sized clearing amid the towering gum trees had been our home for the past two and a half weeks. Here we had laughed and complained, worked and relaxed, panicked every morning about who was going to be chosen to do the next Bushtucker Trial, eaten and slept. It was hard to imagine that today it would all be over.

Our solitude didn't last long. The other contestants were ushered back in for the announcement of the winner. They looked fantastic, a catwalk of showered, tanned contestants clad in clean, fresh, pressed summer fashions – Jenny Frost of the girl band Atomic Kitten was a true glamourpuss, complete with fake tan. Sheree and I exchanged smiles as they reminded themselves of the decidedly unglamorous campsite they had swopped for the luxury of one of the most sumptuous hotels in Queensland, the Palazzo Versace Hotel in Surfer's Paradise.

Once the cue had been given that we were about to go live, presenters Ant and Dec marched purposefully into position for one last time.

My mother got into parliament when I was six, so various vote counts had, for decades, punctuated my life: local elections, by-elections, general elections, votes for the Tory party leadership and so on.

But now it was me on the ballot paper. Not her.

It was Dec who made the announcement.

'The winner of *I'm a Celebrity* 2005 and the new Queen of the Jungle is' – then there was a pause which seemed to go on for ever – '*Carol Thatcher!*'

Wow! Me! This was one of the biggest pinch-yourself-it's-really-happening moments of my life. There is no feeling like winning.

I congratulated Sheree, the runner-up, and the other contestants cheered and clapped.

'I couldn't have done it without all you guys,' I told them all. I hope I sounded sincere, because I really meant it. At the start they had all been contestants chasing viewers' votes, but now, two and a half weeks on, I simply treasured the camaraderie of the group.

Ant and Dec continued, 'That's it. Carol Thatcher is the winner. But before we chat to her, Sheree will be joining us in the studio for a chat in a couple of minutes.'

All the contestants were ushered over a couple of swing bridges which crossed a leafy ravine, and escorted to the studio.

Momentarily, I felt like Bill McKay, the character played by Robert Redford in the film *The Candidate*. Having just won election to the US Senate, he grabs one of his aides and asks, 'What do we do now?'

My memory rewound to three weeks earlier when I'd arrived in Australia . . .

Outside the airport I was met by the local paparazzi. 'Who do you think will win?' had been their recurring question.

'One of the young, glam telly stars,' I'd replied. In the weeks before the show I'd looked up my fellow junglies on Google and seen that they were all public figures – Tony Costa of boy band Blue and Jenny Frost of Atomic Kitten had enormous fan bases, while Jimmy Osmond of the Osmond Brothers had a following of millions.

I'd been certain that I, as the only rank amateur, would be among the first to go. So confident, in fact, that I'd booked a fantastic backpacking trip through Asia to Angkor Wat in Cambodia, then on to Vietnam, before hitting the temples of Bagan on the banks of the Irrawaddy river in Burma.

Three weeks on, and here I was, Queen of the Jungle . . . It was hard to take in what that meant, as I waited to resurface into the real world.

A floor manager brought me back to earth by telling me that the show was in a short commercial break and that I'd have to sprint to the studio to get ready for my live interview and my coronation!

I had already packed the few personal belongings we'd been allowed to bring (swimsuit and so on) and, most important of all, the diary I'd kept, scribbled in charcoal (often warmed and softened by the fire) on any scraps of paper I could lay my hands on. Should I, I wondered, tidy up my little space in the camp, or leave it looking like the informal jungle doss house it had become in the last twenty-four hours, when I had definitely begun to feel demob happy? All of a sudden the area that had been our entire world began fading into the background.

One's perspective from inside the goldfish bowl (whatever form it may take) is vastly different from that of people looking in. Now I was about to find out what the viewers of *I'm a Celebrity* had been seeing on their screens.

During the last few days I'd several times been asked in the Bush Telegraph (an interview booth a few metres from the campsite) why I thought people were voting for me. When interviewing my mother for *Diary of an Election*, my book about the 1983 election campaign, I'd asked her, 'What, as Britain's first woman prime minister, have you brought to the job?' Her reply, 'I'm not the person to answer that question,' had taught me a valuable lesson: never be afraid to pass decisions to others.

I didn't know why people were voting for me. It was their choice, not mine, and in the Bush Telegraph I said so. What I did know, however, was that I was very grateful for their support.

Anyway, now we knew the result, and Sheree, with Ant and Dec, was on set listening to what her fellow celebs had to say about her.

Jimmy Osmond mentioned her gloriously infectious, cackling laugh, Jilly praised her as a natural, charming person, while I said that she was completely the reverse of what you expected from a very glam footballer's wife – she's married to Premiership footballer Harry Kewell – and added, 'I take my hat off to her.'

Then it was my turn. What did the other celebs think of Thatch?

David Dickinson: 'What can you say about Carol? She's a cracking girl and she really is a character.'

Jilly – with whom I'd done the show's memorable Bushtucker Eating Trial – trilled, 'Carol is absolutely daft as a brush, as mad as a hatter.'

Given my cue, I barged onto the set, telling myself not to fall over any cables, or collide with cameras or cameramen, and to concentrate. This wasn't the time to get it wrong.

Ant and Dec took charge. 'Sit yourself up there,' they said, pointing to a large wooden throne. 'How does it feel?'

'I said the other day that if I won I would be amazed, astonished and gobsmacked, and I'm all three of those to the power of a hundred,' I replied.

Then I watched a video of my jungle highlights which, as it was the first time I'd seen anything, was a bit of a revelation. There was a clip from the Skydiving (fortunately before I threw up halfway down); and one from the Bushtucker Trial, during which I asked Ant and Dec if one of the sheets of paper they were holding was the wine list. Then, 'Sorry about the car,' I shrieked, dangling high above a ravine at the bottom of which lay my scarlet toy car, a pile of very bent metal – I only hoped I hadn't handed a pile of ammunition to the anti-women-drivers lobby.

Ant and Dec asked me about life in the jungle and how I'd coped. I told them I'd thoroughly enjoyed it. I was very lucky with my fellow celebs; they were a harmonious group – most of them are in show business so they quite liked talking about each other twenty-three and a half hours a day (I meant this as a compliment). I heard some wonderful yarns and I had a thoroughly good time.

Then I recalled something my mother's PA, Crawfie, used to say: 'Don't look back – you're not going there.' So I looked to the future and continued, 'I don't think you'll have any difficulty recruiting people for the next show, because we all look as if we've enjoyed it.'

Ant and Dec: 'Have you enjoyed your time in camp?'

Thatch: 'I think it has been a life-enhancing experience . . . In previous series people have left early 'cos they didn't like it; there have been rows. But in this programme – thanks to my fellow campers – we replaced acrimonious bickering with amusing banter. And I have to thank everybody else who signed up for this show for coming into it with a generosity of spirit, a pragmatism and a determination to put a lot into it and get a lot out of it. I think as a team we've achieved exactly that.'

Ant and Dec: 'Well done, Carol. And now it's the moment we've been waiting for – to crown the new Queen of the Jungle. And to do the honours, please welcome our very own Jungle Princess, Miss Tara Palmer-Tomkinson.'

Miss P-T looked glitzy and supermodel-stunning, making me deeply aware of how grotty my bright-red ski socks, dusty boots and creased khaki gear looked.

My crown certainly looked sufficiently Jungle-like – full of rope strands, coiled vines and accessorised with samples of Jungle greenery. The biggest surprise was that it fitted my head perfectly.

I knew I would never, ever feel as good as the moment when Tara placed the cane-and-rope Jungle coronet on my head.

Chapter Two

SMALL FRY

IT WAS 13 AUGUST 1953, a sunny Thursday in London, and my
mother decided to go shopping. When she returned to their
Chelsea flat, she found a note from her husband, Denis,
informing her that he'd gone to watch the cricket at the Oval,
which is where he planned to spend the next few days.

As Mum was seven months pregnant and didn't feel a hundred
per cent, she took herself off to Queen Charlotte's Hospital in
west London for a check-up, leaving a note for Denis. The 'baby'
wasn't expected until the end of September, and she hadn't felt
well the entire pregnancy, so she wasn't too concerned by the
strange sensations she was having that day.

By a curious coincidence, that date, 13 August, was also the date on which, eight years later, the citizens of Berlin awoke to find that the checkpoints between East and West were closed and that during the night barbed-wire fences had been put up between the two sectors. This was the beginning of the division of Berlin, in whose reunification Mum, together with Ronald Reagan and Mikhail Gorbachev, was to play such an important part.

Her first shock on arrival at the hospital and being X-rayed was to be told that she was expecting twins. The second: that we were imminent. After a Caesarean section on 15 August, Mark and I were born about three o'clock in the afternoon. He came first and I followed two minutes later.

It took a few hours for Dad to catch up with the news that he was a father. A rugby referee, avid golfer and keen follower of cricket, he had other things on his mind. The end of the forty-first Ashes test series was drawing to a close. After matches at Trent Bridge, Lord's, Old Trafford and Headingley the last was being played at the Oval. It was a momentous time for any cricket fan. (England went on to win the series by two wickets and claim the Ashes for the first time in almost twenty years.)

He got home at the end of the third day's play, found Mum's note and rushed to Queen Charlotte's. He was met by the matron. 'Your wife is in that room,' she told him, pointing down a corridor. 'The babies are in that one.'

'What do you m-mean "babies"?' Dad stammered.

In the matter-of-fact way favoured by hospital personnel, he was informed that Mrs Thatcher had been delivered of twins.

Introduced to us straight away, he was anything but bowled over. He took one look and gasped, 'My God, they look like rabbits! Put them back.'

Our birth came as even more of a surprise because there was no record of twins in either family. Mum and Dad had to rush around and buy another of everything, because they'd got only one. Years later, I read a report in a newspaper which quoted Mum as saying how much Dad – with the benefit of hindsight – regretted that they hadn't insured against the possibility.

There are two questions I have been asked constantly throughout my life. The first is 'What is it like to be a twin?' and the second is 'What's it like to have a famous mum?' As I have always been a twin, and for most of my life my mother has been in the headlines, I defer to the answer she gave whenever she was asked what it was like to be the first female prime minister: 'I don't know – I've never experienced the alternative.'

Mark and I were born in the final year of post-war rationing, which ended at midnight on 4 July 1954. Although of course I can't remember anything of the powdered egg era, with clothing coupons and restrictions on the sale of many items, my mother often told us about her childhood in Grantham, Lincolnshire. During the war, she said, her family would gather round the wireless for the news and to hear Churchill's historic speeches. Whenever the air-raid sirens wailed, the whole Roberts family would shelter under a particularly sturdy dining-room table. One Sunday when the preacher joined them for supper, my grandmother opened a tin of Spam and a can of fruit salad – both special treats. Mum also told her incredulous children that she'd never tasted bananas or grapes until after the war.

After they got married, my parents' first home was my father's old bachelor pad on the sixth floor of a block called Swan Court, Flood Street, just off the King's Road in Chelsea. It had been ideal for Dad when he returned from his wartime stint as a major in the Royal Engineers and became managing director of the Atlas Preservative Company, originally founded in New Zealand by his grandfather, but it wasn't big enough for twins and a full-time nanny. The solution was to rent the flat next door and move us in there, with an inter-connecting door between the two apartments. As soon as we got to tricycle age, the extra space provided an improvised racetrack. With no garden for us to play in, Nanny was instructed to take us twice a day to nearby Ranelagh Gardens for some fresh air.

Mark and I were christened on 13 December 1953, our parents' second wedding anniversary, in John Wesley's Methodist chapel in the City, where they had been married. My mother didn't believe in superstition and never considered the number thirteen unlucky. As she always said, she was born on the thirteenth, married on it, and had us christened on it. And she hasn't done too badly.

Nor, being pragmatic, did horoscopes matter to her. When she was prime minister and the newspapers reported that President Reagan's wife, Nancy, regularly consulted an astrologer about his schedule, Mum was asked in the House of Commons whether she, too, was in thrall to the stargazers. She jumped up off the front bench and told the MP that she was a Libran, adding emphatically, 'a very well-balanced sign'. I myself am a Leo, and if I don't like my horoscope in one tabloid I nip out and buy another paper to see if that one's an improvement. I never buy a third in case it advises me not to throw money around!

Somehow, even as a new mother of twins, Mum found time during her two-week stay in the hospital after our birth to plan the next stage of her career. As she wrote in *The Path to Power*, 'To be a mother and a housewife is a vocation of a very high kind. But I simply felt that it was not the whole of my vocation. I knew that I also wanted a career.' She cited a much-loved quote by Irene Ward, MP: 'While the home must always be the centre of one's life, it should not be the boundary of one's ambitions.'

Having both parents working was the exception in the 1950s and '60s, but it was the norm in the Thatcher family. It was a thoroughly modern partnership and way ahead of its time. Looking back, I am in awe of how they did it. They left the nitty-gritty of running a household and caring for twins to our redoubtable nanny. Neither of my parents was hands-on in the way that successive generations have become. I don't think they can have relished being in charge on nanny's day off. One day when Mark and I were being particularly hideous on the way home from a holiday, my father made that clear. 'For God's sake, teach the children some manners,' he instructed the nanny. Like so many of his generation, he had no intention of getting involved himself.

In 1957, when we were four, my parents purchased a white-washed house in an acre of land in Farnborough, Kent, so that we could have a garden to play in. It was called Dormers, was set amid woods and fields, and became our happy family home for the next decade. More than forty years after we'd left, I returned to Dormers to make a short feature for a BBC television programme about our childhood home. As is often the way, everything seemed to have shrunk.

Both my parents were fanatical gardeners and they transformed the plot on which the house stood. As my father was in the paint, chemical and weed-killer business, he was an expert on – and quite obsessive about – the state of the lawns. Daisies became Public Enemy Number One and were zapped with military precision; the grass mown in perfect stripes. As Dad was such a cricket fan, he put up a practice net and spent hours bowling at Mark. Also bicycle-mad, Mark and I dashed up and down the private avenue from our house to visit neighbouring families with children the same age. The house next door had a swimming pool, which we were sometimes invited to use.

When my mother wasn't reading legal briefs, she pored over bulb catalogues. As with everything she put her mind to, she tackled the garden with extraordinary efficiency. Before long, we had a sensational array of dahlias in one bed, impressive roses, and, in a filled-in pond (so that we didn't accidentally drown), a blaze of scarlet salvias. Walking around the garden all those decades later, looking for clues to my childhood playground, I felt like an archaeologist discovering a prized piece of mosaic whenever I spotted paths she'd planned or flowerbeds she'd planted. The current owners of Dormers showed me a framed letter from her, which they had hung in their hallway. They had written to her expressing concern about the possibility of extending nearby Biggin Hill airport, and this was her reply. (The annual air show at Biggin Hill had always been a day of excitement in the Thatcher household; we watched the planes taking off on television and then sprinted outside to see them fly over.) My mother responded in her usual diplomatic way, adding, 'I never expected to be in correspondence with my old home!'

While Mum commuted to her chambers in Lincoln's Inn every day, Dad drove to his office in Erith. Ordinary family life was inevitably sacrificed because they were both so busy, further complicated by Dad's off-duty passion as a keen rugby football referee. He was often away at matches on a Saturday, returning home with a bagful of muddy kit which my mother dutifully washed. I remember looking at him and thinking, 'I'd get into an awful lot of trouble if I came home as muddy as that.'

My father was a lifelong gin drinker and, until he cut down in his eighties, a heavy smoker. My mother never complained, but it did amuse me how often she used to buy the wrong duty-free cigarettes! He hated 'unusual' food, especially garlic and fried onions, and detested cooking smells wafting through the house. 'Close the kitchen door!' he would yell.

When we ate out, if Dad thought his beef was too rare he'd

summon a waiter, stick his fork into it and go 'moo', which used to make Mark and me giggle. If it was lamb chops in front of him, he'd vary the tactic and explain ever so courteously to the waiter that he couldn't possibly eat them because he'd still be able to taste the wool. The chops would then commute back and forth to the kitchen until charred to Dad's satisfaction. I once suggested to Mum that she should call the restaurant the day before to ask them to get Dad's steak under the grill immediately.

At home we ate well and conventionally rather than terribly adventurously – although my mother would run to a lobster flan or fancy French dessert for occasional buffet parties. To her, food was fuel. It was a case of fill up the tank and get back to work – anything she could make quickly and could be eaten speedily was favoured. One night at Dormers, she was working away and remembered that we would expect an evening meal. She turfed a chicken into the oven but, in her haste, turned on the grill. Before long, the kitchen was full of smoke and the chook grilled to cinders on top and raw underneath.

Once ensconced in Downing Street, she stocked up the freezer in the flat with copious boil-in-the-bag options, which involved immersing a bag of food in boiling water to heat up, snipping open the plastic envelope once done, and decanting onto a plate. Working alone one night, she dumped one of these into a saucepan full of boiling water and went back to work. The telephone rang some time later. It was someone downstairs asking if she was all right. 'Why?' she asked. Then she noticed that the place reeked. Completely forgetting her supper, she had allowed the water to boil dry. Her duck *à l'orange* was cremated, while the charred bottom of the pan was about to succumb to the gas flame.

In contrast to my father, my mother drank sparingly – a gin and tonic or the occasional weak Scotch and soda. Whenever I asked her when Sunday lunch would be, she'd reply, 'Just let me have the other half,' sipping her drink on the few occasions I remember her sinking into an armchair and relaxing.

At twenty-three, she had been the youngest ever female Tory candidate (for Dartford, Kent) when Dad had first met her on a blind date. She put her political career on ice while Mark and I were very young, but in 1958 was adopted as the Conservative candidate for the safe seat of Finchley and Friern Barnet in north-west London. My father was on one of his regular business trips to Africa at the time. Over the years, I have often had to catch up with family news courtesy of the media and it was the same for Dad. Changing planes in Kano, Nigeria, he found an old copy of the *Evening Standard* on the seat next to his. One small paragraph gave him the good news, and he ordered a celebratory gin and tonic.

The following summer we went on a family holiday to Seaview in the Isle of Wight, a routine which continued for a number of years. It was always an adventure from the second we left home, the boot of the car crammed with buckets and spades, cricket bats and beach balls, as we drove to the ferry at Southampton. Mark and I would sit in the back, whining, 'Are we there yet?' That first year we stayed at the old-fashioned Pier Hotel, right on the seafront, but for following summers we rented a small flat. I would be despatched early in the morning to collect freshly baked bread for breakfast, and to buy rolls which Mum filled for picnics.

Seaview was full of boats and dinghies bobbing on their moorings. The yacht club hosted events and laid on terrific firework displays. We had sailing lessons and used to watch the Admiral's Cup competitors as they sailed past the Needles. One memorable summer Dad hired a small motorboat named *Truant*, in which we chugged around, exploring coves. I had my eye on rather grander ocean-going vessels, the Cunard liners, *Queen Mary* and *Queen Elizabeth*, which passed by as they made their way into Southampton at the completion of another trans-Atlantic crossing. I delighted in spotting *Elizabeth* (which had two red funnels) and *Mary* (three), whooping with joy as the large waves they created crashed onto the shingle beach what seemed like an age later. I imagined those on board living glamorous lives and fervently hoped that one day I could be a passenger on one of those magnificent vessels. I was thrilled many years later when Cunard asked me to be a guest speaker on *QE2*.

Back home, we spent the rest of our school holidays going on outings to London. One favourite trip was a visit to Big Ben – when I was much older and acquired my first mobile phone, I chose its distinctive 'bongs' as my ring tone. I remember climbing the spiral staircase to the top of the tower in time to hear the noon chimes. The tour guide advised us to walk on the flat of our foot rather than on tiptoe because it was less tiring. It is a tip I have used ever since. We did a tour of the clock's mechanism, the highlight of which was walking behind the four clock dials, each of them more than twenty-feet high and containing more than three hundred pieces of glass. We felt Lilliputian in comparison to the giant hands on the other side. When the huge hammer struck the Great Bell it was a truly dramatic moment. Little did I know then how much Big Ben and the Houses of Parliament would dominate our lives in the years to come.

Mark was sent to boarding prep school when he was eight. There wasn't much point in running a household for one child, so I was sent to Mymwood, the prep school to Queenswood school, near Hatfield in Hertfordshire, aged nine. Our old nanny returned in the school holidays to housekeep. My mother, who had grown up in a frugal and very purposeful household, told me when I was grown up that she had wanted her children to have the opportunities she hadn't had. So we had riding lessons (I never took to equestrian sport, twigging early on that horses bite at one end and kick at the other) and other extras.

As her own childhood had been extremely regimented, when it came to being a mother herself she favoured a much more flexible approach, giving Mark and me the opportunity to make up our own minds. That meant anything from being allowed to choose the wallpaper in our bedrooms (which she always decorated herself) to church being optional each Sunday.

At Christmas in 1961 we went on a skiing holiday to Lenzerheide in Switzerland. While Mark and I enrolled in ski school, Mum and Dad had private lessons. It was quite brave of them to take up skiing at thirty-five and forty-six respectively, I always thought. Mum was extremely cautious, however, favouring technique over speed. She had no intention of returning home with the nuisance of a leg in plaster. The Ski Club of Great Britain held regular races for children and, being an MP, Mum was asked to present the prizes. I had won a cup and when she moved along the line of winners and was about to present it to me, I hissed through gritted teeth, 'Shake my hand! Shake my hand!' – I was terrified that she might be maternal and even kiss me in public, I just wanted to be like everyone else. The ski trip was such a success that we returned there every Christmas and New Year for five consecutive years. Those, my first overseas holidays, sparked in me a lifelong passion for travel, something my workaholic mother neither shared nor understood, much preferring to stay home and 'get on'.

And get on she did, rising through the political ranks. Her workload increased dramatically and her daily routine usually saw her up at seven o'clock, making breakfast (she insisted we always had a cooked breakfast) while reading through the papers, followed by domestic organisation, then the drive to the House of Commons to deal with votes, constituency matters and her terrifying influx of mail. She might perhaps manage a quick visit to the bank or the hairdresser before dashing to catch a train for an out-of-town political engagement, then back to the House for Prime Minister's Questions, and possibly a late-night sitting.

Her motto was 'Never a wasted moment', and even when she sat under the drier at the hairdresser, while other women were having a manicure or relaxing, she would have a pile of political papers on her knee and work away with characteristic urgency. When she got home in the evenings, she would cook us supper (often still with her coat on), then labour into the small hours, psyching herself up for any speech and scanning reports for the statistics she'd need to ram home a particular point. Rummaging through her handbag, she'd whip out a piece of paper, probably a used House of Commons envelope or the back of a menu, on which she had earlier scribbled a few key phrases.

She always got up early to press her clothes and don one of her famous hats, checking that everything looked immaculate. Waiting to make a speech or greet a visiting VIP, she'd decline offers to sit down. 'I can't. It'll crease my dress' was her standard excuse.

My father was always amazed at how much effort Mum put into everything, especially her speeches, claiming she was better 'off the cuff'. She still somehow found time to paint every room at Dormers, do a weekly bake each Saturday, and to start her lifelong collection of Crown Derby and silver, attending local auctions in between engagements. Dad was just as busy at work, travelling to South Africa for the month of August each year, always making sure to be back for the rugby season. South Africa was an important market for Atlas Preservatives and a country my father – and then my brother – came to adore. Dad rarely kept in touch with home while overseas; if we were lucky, we might receive a standard postcard with about half a dozen words scrawled on it. Inter-continental calls were difficult, on a time delay and expensive, but even if he'd felt like splashing out he wouldn't have made any – he always hated the telephone.

When he was back in England, he worked as hard as Mum, and often didn't get home until gone nine o'clock. I can only remember going to his office once, after the oil tanker *Torrey Canyon* hit the rocks off Cornwall and started to leak oil, becoming one of the first major environmental disasters. Atlas manufactured the foam used to break up the oil slick, and during the Easter break we went down to see the barrels being filled. Dad seemed to regard us as a bit of a nuisance, telling us keep out of the way, but it was interesting to see where he spent so much of his time, and where more than two hundred staff depended on him to keep the company going. Friends claimed later that Dad was as ambitious for Mum as she was for herself, and that he stayed at work so late and so long because he knew she was busy working, too. Their marriage was truly a meeting of minds.

In an interview with the London *Evening News* in 1960, just before my mother was given her first ministerial position, in the Pensions Department, she elaborated: '[My husband] is every bit as busy as I am, if not more so. Wives whose husbands are in top jobs see very little of them as they work late, have to travel to different parts of the country and sometimes have to go abroad. My husband was on a tour of the Middle East when I made my maiden speech. His busy life would go on whether I was a Member of Parliament or not, and it is rare for him to be at home for more than one evening during the week. Family life is centred around the weekends, when we are at home together and devote most of the time to the children.'

By 1964, however, Dad had pushed himself to the verge of a nervous breakdown. He was given a health warning by a doctor who told him he was making himself ill with overwork. In response, he took a sabbatical and went on a three-month safari to South Africa to convalesce, followed by several weeks at our favourite Swiss ski resort. Stressed and overworked herself, Mum went down with pneumonia while he was away. When Dad returned home, he made the decision to sell Atlas to the Castrol Oil Company, which immediately offered him a job on its board. He'd barely got his feet under the desk when Castrol was taken over by Burmah Oil, the oldest-established British oil company. The security of running a small family company was a distant memory, and he told Mum fearfully, 'I probably won't have a job, love.' He couldn't have been more wrong. Burmah appointed him senior divisional director, a job he took to like a duck to water. Selling Dormers, Mum and Dad kept a flat in London and bought The Mount, a mock-Tudor house in Lamberhurst, Kent, dividing their time between the two.

During my teens, the Swinging Sixties rather passed me by, chiefly because – during the summer weekends – the television was permanently switched to the latest cricket match for the viewing pleasure of Dad and Mark. Outvoted, I would retreat to my room to sing along to Cliff Richard's *Summer Holiday*. I also liked the Beatles and was an avid fan of pirate radio stations, twiddling and turning the dial on my humble, crackly transistor to pick up Radio Caroline or Radio Luxembourg. Much to my parents' chagrin, I took to wearing an old fireman's greatcoat from an army-surplus store and an enormously long scarf which I had knitted myself.

My greatest passion, though, was the movies. I went to the cinema as often as I could, marvelling especially at Audrey Hepburn's success with her elocution lessons in the musical *My Fair Lady*. I have never managed to pronounce my Rs correctly, however much I persevered with elocution exercises like 'Round the ragged rocks the ragged rascal ran.' I was a gawky teenager, and the vision of Miss Hepburn dressed for a ball and speaking beautifully was my image of perfection. I was also a big fan of 007 and would bore everyone about how sensational I thought Oddjob's stunt of decapitating a statue with his bowler hat was in *Goldfinger*. I couldn't hear enough of John Barry's high-octane score and Shirley Bassey's rendition of the title song. I lapped up *Dr Zhivago*, *The Sound of Music*, *Butch Cassidy and the Sundance Kid*. I'd seen *Diamonds Are Forever* so often, I could almost recite Blofeld's lines. Bambi and Thumper, the film's lethal gymnasts, inspired me – in a (hopeless) attempt to become svelter – to attend a few aerobics classes. I even dragged my mother to see *Those Magnificent Men in Their Flying Machines*, and *Mayerling*, starring Omar Sharif and Catherine Deneuve, at the end of which Mum wept, much to my embarrassment.

Occasionally, my mother's status did mean family perks but the one that I felt had real 'Wow!' factor actually came via a contact of Dad's. Would the whole family like to go to the London premiere of the film *Waterloo*, starring Christopher Plummer and Rod Steiger? he asked.

Not half.

Always useless with clothes (to my mother's despair), I whizzed off and purchased a long dress and fancy shoes for the premiere. On the red carpet at the Odeon Leicester Square, as flash-lights popped, I was agog. I'd never thought this kind of thing would happen to me. Sadly, I couldn't persuade Dad to share my enthusiasm. He had his feet far too firmly on the ground to consider show business anything other than phoney. He was disgusted when one famous star walked in and, seeing that the TV interviewer was already engaged, went out again to make a second, better entrance.

Following the throng out of the auditorium after the film, I spotted one of its stars. 'Look, that's Rod Steiger!' I hissed to Mum, my heart pounding.

'Who? I wouldn't know what he looked like,' she replied flatly.

'But you've just spent the last three hours watching him on a giant screen!' Then I realised that she had probably spent most of the film catching up on some much-needed sleep.

Less than a month before my sixteenth birthday, I sat spellbound in front of a different screen, that of our television, like millions of others around the world, to watch the Apollo 11 landing on the moon. It was July 1969, and this was far better than any fictional film. We watched the entire saga as a family in open-mouthed wonder as Neil Armstrong and Buzz Aldrin touched down in their lunar module, *Eagle*, among the shadows, rocks and craters.

Neil Armstrong climbed down the steps of the ladder, jumping the last few feet to become the first man on the moon. He then uttered his memorable words: 'That's one small step for man, one giant leap for mankind.'

Little did I know that, soon, my mother would be trailblazing similarly – in her own unique way.

Chapter Three

HAPPY TRAILS

GENERAL ELECTIONS PUNCTUATE the lives of politicians' children in the same way rehearsals and first nights provide the framework to those whose parents are in the theatre. The drama of it soon becomes a way of life.

There are other parallels, too: defeat for an MP on polling day is one of the most publicly humiliating ways to be summarily dismissed from a job. It's comparable to damning first-night reviews resulting in the embarrassingly premature closure of a much-hyped show.

I lived through nine general elections between the ages of six and thirty-two, from 1959, when my mother first became an MP, until 1987, her final campaign as Tory leader. Looking back, I remain eternally grateful that, if it was my fate to have an ambitious politician for a mother, at least it was on this side of the Atlantic Ocean rather than in the United States. Our election campaigns last for just three weeks, whereas the US system, with its interminable primaries, Super Tuesday, conventions and scandals, seemingly spans years before the actual vote. (What is civilised, though, in the USA is the timetable after the election: the new president gets from November until the inauguration in January to prepare for taking office, thus leaving the departing president a last Christmas and New Year in the White House and plenty of time to say farewell to Camp David.)

As was so often the case, it was my father who had the best perspective on the entire general election process: 'Why we have to go through this carry-on for three bloody weeks is beyond me,' he said. 'After all, it's either "Hello, it's me again," or "Goodbye."' As a grown-up, I tended to agree. But I was only six years old when my mother was elected to parliament.

Mark and I had been quite bewildered by all the fuss of the political campaign, although we did pick up the jargon – words such as 'three-line whip', 'divisions', 'pairs', 'constituency' and 'constituents' were soon added to our growing vocabulary. The election had been announced while we were on holiday on the Isle of Wight, a fact which, I am sure, must have ruined the break for my mother.

Although Finchley had a comfortable Tory majority, Mum set about her campaign as if it were a marginal. Whatever the strains and stresses of being a candidate while working full-time and juggling being a wife and mother, she never brought them home, and ran the house with characteristic efficiency. She drew on her experience of having fought Dartford twice in the 1950s. Later, she recalled, in a newspaper interview: 'It takes time before you know what to worry about and what not to. You know you can cope, and stamina comes with experience, and then the accumulated experience takes you through because you've seen it all before and you learn not to get depressed about something which would knock a less experienced person rather hard.'

Her energy was bottomless as she commuted across London from Kent in her blue Ford Anglia to her constituency office in Finchley, to canvass and speak. The London *Evening News* was spot-on with a feature about Mum headlined, 'Mrs Thatcher Is the Type Who Can Cope.'

On election day, Mark and I were shuttled to our respective schools by friends' mothers. Our house was full of election paraphernalia like loud-hailers and manifesto leaflets. We had no idea how momentous that night would be. While we slept, my mother was elected, increasing the Tory majority by three thousand five hundred to an extremely comfortable sixteen thousand.

The following morning, after only a few hours' sleep, the new MP for Finchley was in the kitchen, preparing breakfast as usual, and seeing us off. As I waited in my uniform to be collected for school, my satchel slung over my shoulder, she came to the front porch and said, 'Do go and have a look at the car, before we take everything off.'

I ran across our crunchy gravel drive and struggled with the heavy garage doors. I prised one open, the sunlight flooded in and I gasped. The humble little Ford Anglia was in fancy-dress: festooned with Tory-blue streamers, balloons, and a 'Vote Thatcher' poster bearing a photograph of my mother. I was mystified. What was she doing on what looked like a WANTED notice out of a cowboy film? On the roof of the car was an enormous loud-hailer. Here was the reason she'd almost lost her voice and was popping throat pastilles at a rate I'd never been allowed to guzzle sweets.

'My mummy's very important. She's an MP,' I crowed to my schoolfriends, while my six-year-old brain tried to connect the pieces of the jigsaw – the car that looked like a circus prop, and a place called the House of Commons, about which all I could remember was that it had green leather seats. First, my mother had been a chemist, then she was a barrister. Now, she was an MP – one of only twelve women compared to three hundred and fifty male Conservatives in the Commons – and our lives would now be on a permanent political rollercoaster.

To begin with, though, nothing much changed. She still organised the household and gave daily instructions to our nanny. We still went on family holidays to the Isle of Wight and Switzerland. She made all our birthday cakes, often shaped like trains or cars and intricately iced; she attended parents' evenings and speech days at school (although she'd sit in the car going through constituency papers until the final moment). She even knitted (because Nanny did, so Mum wanted to make us jumpers too). Both she and my father had always worked, always been busy, so we didn't yet have a sense of the remarkable journey we were all about to make, although perhaps my mother secretly suspected all along.

Successive election campaigns punctuated our lives every four or so years as we grew up. In 1964, two years after my brother and I started boarding school, our mother was campaigning again. That was the year when Harold Wilson edged the Conservatives out of office (he increased his parliamentary majority with a landslide swing in 1966). For the next five years Mum was shuffled around a variety of shadow cabinet posts I usually read about in the papers while at school. At an early party conference in Blackpool her speech in the taxation debate impressed a political journalist on the *Sun*, whose headline ran: 'A Fiery Blonde Warns of the Road to Ruin'. The article said, 'Mrs Margaret Thatcher, the pretty blonde MP for Finchley, got a standing ovation for one of those magnificent fire-in-the-belly speeches which are heard so seldom.'

I remember her pace of life being perpetually busy. She once confirmed it to a journalist: 'There are twenty-four hours in a day and if you fill them with activity your mind is always active and you're not thinking of yourself, you're just getting on with whatever you have to do next.'

We would come home during the holidays to find her sitting at the kitchen table with piles of *Hansard*s (the official report of proceedings in both Houses), along with her usual mountain of correspondence. Nothing could distract her. One night when Mark and I were watching *Top of the Pops*, and she was sitting nearby, working her way through a pile of papers and constituents' letters, I asked, 'Is the television disturbing you, Mum?'

She didn't answer so I repeated the question – twice.

Finally, she looked up. 'Pardon, dear? The TV? Oh, I didn't realise it was on.'

Once, when the mother of a friend of mine was discussing the arrangements for getting us together during the school holidays, Mum declared that a particular date was unsuitable because she'd be 'in the House'.

'Oh, so shall I,' replied the other mother, thinking it odd to state the obvious.

Mum, of course, missed it. No other house registered with her except the House of Commons.

Inevitably, just as kids with parents in the film business make a lot of visits to the set and backlots, I did a fair amount of hanging out at Westminster. I became familiar with the menu in the Members' Canteen in the House of Commons. As a treat in the summer, we were allowed strawberries and cream, sitting at a table on the vast terrace in the lee of Big Ben, overlooking the Thames and Westminster Bridge. Leaning over the wall, I'd gaze at the river endlessly, fascinated by the swirls and eddies, as that huge body of water raced by, oblivious to the daily goings-on. Then, suddenly, I'd hear her voice telling me to snap out of it and we'd be off. I was already accustomed to trying to keep up with my mother, who walked not just briskly but at nearly jogging tempo through St Stephen's Entrance, down the steps of the massive Westminster Hall with its colossal oak hammer-beam roof. While she sat and dictated replies to letters from constituents in an office shared with a number of MPs' secretaries, I doodled on House of Commons notepaper or read until it was time to go out and wait in the taxi queue in New Palace Yard.

I often used to sit and wait for her on one of the bottle-green leather seats in the Central Lobby – a huge octagonal 'crossroads' between the House of Commons and Lords. Because I was still small, my feet didn't touch the ground. I used to gaze up at the enormous mosaics of Britain's patron saints: St George, St David, St Andrew and St Patrick. My perch was an excellent spot for people-watching as MPs bustled about their business. I was always a tad disappointed when they disappeared into the post office on one side of the Central Lobby, which seemed such an ordinary thing to do. Weren't they supposed to be running the country?

I often watched the Speaker's procession passing through the Central Lobby on the way to the Chamber of the House of Commons. It was all very impressive to a child. At the start of each day's business, the Speaker enters the House, preceded by the serjeant-at-arms carrying a glittering golden mace. His staff wear silk, damask, tights and buckled court shoes. When they enter the

33

Central Lobby, one of the uniformed policemen bellows, 'Hats off, strangers!' It so hit the mark as a piece of theatre that I used to pass up the opportunity to go to pantomimes with friends – after all, I'd seen men in tights before.

Of course, there were perks to having an MP in the family. I loved the State Opening of Parliament, and remember the first time I saw the Queen arriving in her gold carriage with all the accompanying pageantry. I loved the other glitz and ceremonials, too, and saw them at much closer range than most people, from the Royal Gallery (through which the Queen processes on her way to the House of Lords) and once from a visitors' gallery inside the Chamber itself.

I was intrigued by the spectacle of the lords in their crimson robes – a vision of grandeur to make anyone blink, particularly mid-morning. I loved revolving my eyeballs to spot an earl – three rows of ermine trim on his robe – or a duke (four). I became a bit of a junior anorak on the event, and would bore any schoolfriend who would listen with the details of how, before every State Opening of Parliament, the Yeomen of the Guard search the cellars. They have done so ever since the Gunpowder Plot conspirators tried to blow parliament up on the day of the State Opening in 1605.

When I complained once to my mother that she wasn't like my friends' mothers, who didn't work and were always at home, she stopped what she was doing (making pancakes) to tell me pragmatically, 'Darling, you have to understand that you have a lot of benefits that other children don't have: you can come to the State Opening of Parliament and have supper at the House of Commons.'

By the time I was sixteen, she had been an MP for more than a decade and now she was campaigning for my fourth general election, so I was well versed in the business of electioneering. On the final night, we were heading home in Dad's car on a perfect June evening. Mum had visited the polling stations in her constituency, and the car radio was broadcasting election news. All the indications were that Harold Wilson's Labour government would be returned to office and that Tory leader Ted Heath would remain in opposition.

Sitting in the back, I was counting the weeks until the end of term, only half paying attention to the spiel coming over the airwaves. Then the mood in the car suddenly changed when Mum heard the results of an early exit poll. 'If that's right, we've won,' she blurted out.

I could hear the excitement and anticipation in her voice. If the predictions were true, she could be on the verge of upgrading from a shadow cabinet minister to a seat in the Cabinet Room in Number Ten, under the gaze of Robert Walpole, whose portrait hangs over the fireplace. Was it possible? Could she soon be filling Barbara Castle's power heels as one of the few women cabinet members? Mrs Castle was the secretary of state for employment in the Labour government. She had my mother's well-sprayed hair – except hers was very red – she had been to Oxford, and she was petite, dynamic and charismatic. In *A History of Modern Britain* Andrew Marr described her as 'the most effective female politician of the age'.

Only a fairly maverick punter at that time would have dared to bet against Harold Wilson winning his third general election. Throughout the campaign Labour had maintained a pretty constant double-digit lead in the polls. Andrew Marr added that the campaign had pitted 'Wilson's pudgy face and pipe, against Heath's vast manic grin and yacht sailing. There were good reasons for Labour to think that they would see off the Tories yet again . . . the opinion polls were on side and the press was generally predicting an easy Labour victory. Even right-wing commentators lavished praise on Wilson's television performance and mastery of debate, though he pursued an avowedly presidential style and tried to avoid controversy.'

In the months leading up to the election, Ted Heath and the shadow cabinet, including my mother, had met for a weekend brainstorming session at the Selsdon Park Hotel, Croydon. A small piece in a gossip column claimed that Mum was caught looking rather guiltily at the gourmet menu, while her family was at home 'fending for themselves and probably surviving on humble sausage-and-mash'. We didn't mind. In those days, Mark and I thought it was quite exciting to get a mention in any newspaper. Little did we know all that was about to change.

Now the polling stations were closing, and as the last electors cast their votes Mum turned up the volume of the car radio so as not to miss a word. After that unexpectedly optimistic prediction over the airwaves, my parents decided to change their plans and head for the Savoy Hotel and the election party being hosted by Lady Pamela Berry. A great political hostess in the bygone style, she was the wife of Lord Hartwell, then proprietor of the *Daily Telegraph*.

Arriving at the Savoy, we were greeted by the very glamorous Lady Pamela, glittering in a long evening dress and dripping with diamonds. I must have had an Alice-in-Wonderland expression. Looking around, I was bowled over by how lavish the scene was. I had never seen anything like it. Waiters circulated, balancing flutes of champagne on serving trays, and platters of sophisticated and tempting canapés were on offer. I asked Dad who the hundreds of guests were. 'The great and the good,' he whispered. There were politicians from all parties, media personalities and establishment figures. Television screens had been installed around the ballroom-sized salon so that the election results could be followed count by count. Various factions grouped themselves into 'huddles' to listen.

The BBC anchorman, Cliff Michelmore, presided over the coverage, interviewing pundits and digesting the views of pollsters before going live to the results of key seats. Prior to this remarkable night, I had always watched the results at home, filling in one of the polling guides the newspapers always publish. Tory gains were notched up and the trend started to indicate that the Labour Party was on the way out. An energising buzz filled the room as the Tory supporters became increasingly hopeful. In sailing parlance, HMS *Great Britain* was changing tack, with a new commodore on the bridge, himself no stranger to the role of ocean-racing skipper. I remember one couple having a furious argument in the corner of a room. The man was rabidly anti-Tory and haranguing his wife for her lack of political passion. 'These people are going to govern your life for the next four years,' he steamed. I wondered what he meant by 'these people'.

I would soon learn just how polarising politics could be, but the vibes that night looked positive. While chatting to me, Andrew Alexander, a financial journalist, suggested that my mother could be the next chancellor of the exchequer. Not a woman, I thought. I was not alone in my view.

When the results had finally been counted, the new members' list featured names, from both sides of the political divide, which would crop up in the headlines for the rest of the century and into the next. They included John Prescott, Neil Kinnock, John Smith, Norman Tebbit and Kenneth Clarke. My mother was appointed secretary of state for education and science in the new cabinet. She came home from the first meeting and told us about a special chair at Number Ten, used formerly by Barbara Castle and now by her, with a protective frill to stop its legs snagging tights. Little did she know what a controversial post she had been given, with the looming issue of grammar schools versus comprehensive schools, and strict budgetary constraints in her department which were to see her described as 'Public Enemy Number One' over free school milk. But, after her years of combating male chauvinism and entrenched views on whether a mother should even consider working, let alone entering politics, she must have had a good idea what she would have to face. It would be a decade before she invented the verb 'handbagging', but she was no novice in battle before that.

Asked in an interview for the *Finchley Press* whether she would like to become the first woman prime minister, she gave a reply which was to haunt her for the next twenty years. 'No,' she said emphatically. 'There will not be a woman prime minister in my lifetime – the male population is too prejudiced.'

It might well have been, but my redoubtable mother managed it anyway.

Chapter Four

SINK OR SWIM

FAMILY LIFE WAS conducted at an urgent pace. No one walked up or down the stairs, they dashed; no one talked calmly, they gabbled. Mum was in her constituency, or in the Commons, or on the campaign trail, or at her government department. Dad was 'reverse' commuting from London to Swindon working for Burmah Oil. Mark and I were studying and working in various part-time jobs, and rushing back and forth from the family home in Flood Street, a couple of hundred yards from the busy King's Road, a stone's throw from where my parents had started married life.

My mother's cabinet lifestyle was much harder and far less glamorous than I'd ever imagined. Our hallway became a left-luggage depot of official red despatch boxes or circular hat-boxes; Mum's favourite hat was a navy-and-white-striped 'humbug' design often caricatured in cartoons. Complete strangers were frequent visitors. There were piles of *Hansards* where most people kept their TV guides. Mum was always whizzing in and out for evening engagements in long dresses. Over a hurried breakfast there would be tantalising mentions of official invitations to Buckingham Palace, Number Ten or Chequers. So preoccupied was she that she fell to calling me by her secretaries' names, working her way through them until she reached 'Carol'. I didn't blame her; they contributed much more than I did to the smooth running of her life.

I was never the Chelsea teenager whose mother waited for her to come home before the decreed curfew. In fact, it was the other way round. One morning when I was woken close to dawn by the horses of the Household Cavalry – whose exercise route included our street – and went down to the kitchen to make a cup of coffee, I found my mother there.

'You're up early,' I remarked sleepily.

'I've just come in,' she corrected me. 'The House sat all night.'

Even when I embarked on my first driving lessons, everything and everyone seemed to be pelting full speed ahead all around me. My instructor, in his wisdom, took me round Sloane Square in the rush hour – one of the most terrifying moments of my life. Inching along, barely achieving forward propulsion as buses overtook me and irritated motorists hooted their horns, I gripped the steering wheel and nearly went off the whole idea. Ever full of advice, my mother volunteered to help with some driving practice. Her stint as shadow minister for transport some years before made her an exacting instructor. Not only was she an absolute stickler for the speed limit but she kept her right hand hovering over the handbrake, ready to yank it up and send me into a tailspin at any moment. Thanks to her, though, I eventually passed my test.

I had no inkling of what it would be like having a member of the family in the cabinet, but I soon found out. Barely three months after the election, there was a dramatic incident when four civilian airliners, carrying more than three hundred passengers to America from Europe, were hijacked by the Popular Front for the Liberation of Palestine, and flown to a remote airstrip in Jordan. During the height of the week-long crisis, I remember my mother going off in evening dress to a dinner and leaving a note propped up against the empty milk bottles on the front step, saying where she was should an emergency arise. This was the days before mobile phones and all slightly DIY.

There were bombs closer to home as well. Between 1970 and 1972, a militant communist group called the Angry Brigade carried out more than twenty terrorist attacks throughout England. In January 1971, they targeted the house of Mum's colleague Robert Carr, secretary of state for employment and productivity. Mum called him immediately and expressed her relief that he and his family were unhurt. 'The most shaking part of the experience,' she told us, 'was the second bomb.' Two had been planted: one near the front door, the second at the back.

From that day on, every time I walked past our dustbins outside the back door, I had my fingers crossed. Later, after outspoken Tory supporter and anti-IRA campaigner Ross McWhirter was shot dead, I became much more security aware and when I bought my first, second-hand car, a policeman advised me to attach a mirror to a pole or broomstick and take a thorough look at the reflection of the underside of my car each time, before I got in. I politely explained that unless the device had 'Bomb' printed on it in giant luminous letters I wouldn't spot it. I didn't have a clue what anything on the underside of a car was meant to look like.

Like most students, I was always short of cash. I took summer jobs picking soft fruit on farms near my parents' home in Lamberhurst, an occupation guaranteed to turn your back into a croquet hoop. In London, I pedalled my rusty old bicycle to casual jobs in bookshops, department stores, or restaurants, where I worked as a waitress. One was a quintessentially English restaurant called Tiddy Doll's Eating House in Shepherd Market, Mayfair, an area which had a reputation for ladies of the night. Finishing work after midnight one night, as I walked back to unchain my bicycle I received an offer from a gentleman on the lookout for female company.

'I'm very flattered, but no, thanks,' I replied cheerily. I could imagine the headlines.

One of my more outlandish student jobs was as a temporary lift operator during the Harrods sales. I first twigged how seriously some people took the twice-yearly sales when, in the days leading up to my first, bargain hunters arrived on reconnaissance. Armed with stopwatches, they dashed around at a near-sprint, dodging customers and displays, working out the quickest route to the item they'd got their eye on.

One asked me if on 'the day', I could take him straight to a specific floor.

'No,' I replied.

'For a fiver?' he asked.

The answer was still the same.

It was with growing apprehension that I waited for opening time on day one of the sale. At nine o'clock on the dot the general manager blew a whistle, all the store's ten doors opened simultaneously, and shoppers swarmed in, resembling the Light Brigade charging with the determination of a rugger scrum. Faced with three hundred thousand customers on that first day alone, the sense of people, people everywhere was overwhelming. Whenever I opened the doors, there was a surge of humanity and it took stamina and authority to restrict numbers to the maximum load.

Engineers estimated that each lift operator drove his or her lift four and a half miles a day, taking customers to the store's four floors. To me, it felt like yo-yoing up and down in a sardine tin while keeping up a non-stop spiel: 'First floor – everything for ladies, babies and brides. Mind the doors, please, going up . . .'

45

The chief consolation was my staff discount. I used to stagger home with the store's distinctive carrier bags loaded with irresistible items, all financed by Mum. It was too much for my brother. 'Do you actually work there, or just shop?' he'd ask sarcastically, while helping himself to my Food Hall goodies.

Mark was certainly the star twin. At school at Harrow he excelled at sport and played for the school's cricket First XI for two consecutive years. My father was inordinately proud when he was selected to play in the Eton–Harrow match at Lord's. His forte was a game called racquets, which I always used to describe as 'a distant cousin of squash'. Mark and his partner won the national public schools championship the year my mother made it into the cabinet.

Other people's more glamorous lives fascinated me, too. The Chelsea Library was minutes from our house and close to the Chelsea Registry office, where I'd gawk at the famous newlyweds posing for photographs in a cloud of confetti. In the library I absorbed every detail of the lives of the jet-setting icons of the 1970s like Aristotle Onassis, Jackie Kennedy and Princess Grace of Monaco. I could have won a TV quiz on what I knew about them.

It was a much-needed distraction. I was a law student at University College, London, during most of Mum's time as minister for education, and it wasn't a particularly comfortable experience. Hers was a controversial portfolio and she certainly made the headlines. The government's decision to end free school milk for children over seven, using the money instead to refurbish existing schools and build new ones, heaped criticism and ridicule on her. She was dubbed 'Thatcher, the Milk Snatcher'. The *Sun* called her, 'The most unpopular woman in Britain', and she became the butt of many a vicious political cartoon. Though she was admired for her toughness and intellect, the consensus was that she was 'out of touch', living in a big house in Kent with a wealthy husband, wearing fancy hats, twinset and pearls, and with nannies and private education for her children.

Despite her tough public persona, the criticism rankled, especially when she thought it was downright unfair. Dad was brilliant at rallying her spirits, and Jean Rook, columnist of the *Daily Express*, told her to fight back. 'Show some spunk, Margaret,' she wrote. 'Remember flaming Barbara Castle when she came back at critics like a blowlamp.' I think Mum must have taken the advice to heart.

There were more controversies to come, not least the battle over grammar schools and myriad issues about pay with the National Union of Teachers, not to mention student grants. Because of my conflict of interests, I had to develop a bit of a split personality. To my student contemporaries my mother was the enemy and dozens of anti-Thatcher demonstrations and marches were organised. 'Are you coming, Carol?' they'd ask hopefully. 'We can't remember where her office is.'

Unfortunately, it wasn't only my mother's political policies that made me a target for flak. Feminists didn't think she was doing enough for their cause. This was the era of 'Women's Lib' but my mother was a stratosphere away from the bra-burning demonstrations of the time. On the contrary, she felt the movement had done very little for her. She was a hard-working example of female success from relatively lowly beginnings who had achieved cabinet rank by pragmatically getting on with the task in hand rather than by manning barricades and wasting precious time protesting.

In the face of all the hostility towards her, I developed my own survival mechanism and I stuck to it. For decades when I was asked what I 'felt' about this or that aspect of her politics, I'd reply that I'd given up the extravagance of 'feeling' back in 1970.

Desperate to see more of the world, and happy to escape from all the flak, I was bitten by the travel bug and took off on one of the earliest Eurorail passes, which gave me access to something like twenty countries for twenty quid. Then I went to Israel and worked for a while on a kibbutz, where I seemed to spend most of my time inoculating baby chicks. Later on I took up cycling, and had some memorable trips.

My mother detested holidays and never understood my itchy feet. In fact, I would go as far as to say she was the most unwilling holidaymaker in the world.

Her attitude to travel is perhaps best illustrated by a dinner-party conversation she once had with journalist and columnist Matthew Parris, reported in his autobiography, *Chance Witness*. He explained his plan to spend four months on a remote island in the sub-Antarctic, but was interrupted by my mother. 'I know what you'll be looking for,' she told him. 'You want to go thousands of miles to some remote and dangerous place, climb to the top of a mountain, look up at the moon and stars, and say, "Here I am in a wild and dangerous place, miles from anywhere, looking at the moon and the stars." And it will be worth one newspaper article, or at the most two. And then you'll have to come all the way back again. Now take my advice, dear, don't bother. You can see the moon and the stars from Spalding.'

She took the view that holidays could be counter-productive, mainly because, on her return, any therapeutic value gained from sea or mountain air immediately, and comprehensively, evaporated at the sight of the piles of work which had accumulated in her in-tray during her absence.

Playwright turned speechwriter Ronnie Millar described the annual syndrome best in his book *A View from the Wings*: 'Margaret would reluctantly defer, but, after approximately twenty-four hours of enforced leisure and not a crisis in sight calling for her instant return . . . she tended to grow desperate. The picture of her supposedly lugging Denis's golf clubs round whatever course was adjacent to the holiday home with an expression that says: "I'd like to grab a four-iron and clout whoever talked me into this" is a photo opportunity to be treasured.'

As friends and colleagues left our annual Boxing Day lunch party, they learned not to ask what Mum planned to do with the New Year holiday. They knew the answer. More often than not, she'd reach for a couple of telephone-directory-thick volumes on some aspect of government policy and say how much she was looking forward to getting back to work.

She didn't realise it, but she was about to have much more time on her hands: her days as a cabinet minister were coming to an end. The government's fortunes were anything but flourishing. The Yom Kippur war had resulted in soaring oil prices, and the crisis was compounded by a miners' strike. Ted Heath introduced the disastrous three-day working week. Televisions went off at a set time every night, and the message went out that could all those who didn't want to capitulate to the trade unions please brush their teeth in the dark? We were back in the Dark Ages. Columnists observed that the African colonies we'd granted independence to were doing better than we were.

In the 1974 general election, no single party won an overall majority, although Labour won the largest number of seats. In the aftermath, Mum came into the kitchen while I was watching TV on the possibility of Ted Heath forming a coalition with the Liberals.

'What's going to happen?' I enquired.

'You're not going out, are you?' she asked, and then she said, 'Ted's going to resign.'

I think that was the last bit of inside information I got. At Number Ten, she often started a sentence when I was around (and a journalist) with the disclaimer (and warning), 'You don't know this . . .'

Unable to form the coalition, Ted Heath did indeed resign as

PM, and my mother lost her job. With time on her hands, Dad persuaded her to go on a fortnight's holiday to Corsica, but they were home within a week. 'There wasn't much to see and we've done it,' Mum declared.

I decided to get away, but where to? I was no linguist, so Europe was out. The Antipodes beckoned. After all, there was a Thatcher family precedent: my great-grandfather had headed to New Zealand a century before. Australia particularly appealed: the Sydney Opera House, Ayers Rock, the Great Barrier Reef and the Outback. I bought a piggy bank and began saving, working at shipping law in a City legal firm by day, and doing waitress shifts in a restaurant at night.

But there was another instalment in Maggie's law of politics: the unexpected always happens. In the midst of all the political and personal turmoil, Mum decided to challenge Ted Heath for the party leadership. Keith Joseph had seemed an obvious replacement, and Mum wanted him to stand and would have supported him, but when he chose not to she felt she had no alternative but to stand herself. She would be up against Willie Whitelaw, Geoffrey Howe and Jim Prior, among others. Her friend and colleague Airey Neave, a former member of MI6 who acquired notoriety after a daring break out from Colditz, an infamous prisoner of war camp, agreed to mastermind her campaign, and Mum also recruited Norman Tebbit. I greeted this information about my mother's next career move as a statement of fact. Her decision shocked Dad, although he was tremendously supportive.

Secretly, he worried that, if she polled badly, it would be fatal for her career. As Mum was such a rank outsider, it didn't seem terribly likely that it would happen.

Newspaper coverage about the Thatcher household quadrupled, with political journalists eager to discover everything they could about the surprise new candidate. Unlike the coverage of her male counterparts, there was a great deal of focus on her appearance, including her hats, hair and clothes. Mum agreed to take part in a *World in Action* programme called *Why I Want to Be Leader*, in which her every move (and ours) was scrutinised for a week by television cameras. Prophetically, she told the presenter that Ted Heath had been Tory leader for ten years and that it was 'not a freehold for life'. Trying to emphasise her humble roots, she gave an interview to a magazine for pensioners in which she confided some of her Grantham housekeeping tips such as: stock the larder with tinned food, and take advantage of special offers. This was jumped upon by her opponents, who branded her a hoarder.

Late one evening when Mum was out, the doorbell rang. Dad opened it to find a photographer and a loaded supermarket trolley on the doorstep.

'Would Mrs Thatcher be photographed with it?' he asked hopefully.

'Not here,' came the gruff reply.

'Would you do it instead, as a stand-in?'

Dad muttered the equivalent of 'Not bloody likely!' and closed the door.

Although Mum had entered the leadership contest as the underdog, her substantial win on the first ballot galvanised interest. Airey Neave had done a fine job in rallying the back-benchers in what was later described as 'a peasants' revolt'. Dad – with typical understatement – said he was surprised. He wasn't alone. Perhaps, like many of his generation, he couldn't imagine a woman leading the Tories and aspiring to lead the country. My mother joked that a male victor would make life easier for popular television impersonator Mike Yarwood, but, she added helpfully, if it turned out to be her, 'they could always get Danny La Rue'. It was a brave performance at a time of high risk. Victory would make her the first woman to lead a political party in Britain. Defeat would probably condemn her to political oblivion and accusations of gross disloyalty.

I was in the middle of my exams when my parents' lives took these dramatic turns, so I decamped to a friend's house most days to study and get away from the incessantly ringing phones. On the day of the Tory leadership ballot, I was sitting my finals. 'What's the matter, darling?' my mother asked, seeing me sitting pensively at the breakfast table.

'Today's exam, Mum,' I replied.

'Well, you can't be as nervous as me,' she chided.

I looked up, surprised, and noticed her newly coiffed hair for the first time. Much debate had taken place as to whether the simple act of making the hairdressing appointment that morning might be tempting fate. She had chosen a smart black-and-white outfit. The image of her that morning is engraved on my memory because she coordinated perfectly with the tiles on the floor of our kitchen.

Dad, who was nearly sixty by then, drove his green company Audi down the M4 to work as usual that morning after his breakfast of a half grapefruit, toast and marmalade. Just because his wife might or might not be the new leader of Her Majesty's Opposition by the end of the working day didn't mean he was going to alter his schedule. His secretary of thirty years, Phyllis Kilner (who'd worked for his father, Jack), had his customary cup of coffee waiting.

For me, too, life had to go on as normal. Although, when I handed my exam paper to the invigilator in a cavernous hall behind Marble Arch later that afternoon, he asked me, 'Do you know the result of the ballot?'

'How could I?' I asked incredulously. I'd just spent three hours wrestling with complicated legal principles.

'Your mother won,' he said. My jaw dropped. Christ! This sort of thing didn't happen to people like us. 'There's a photographer and reporter waiting outside for your reaction. Would you rather go out the back exit?'

'Yes,' I replied, dazed.

My father, I discovered later, had learned the news of her victory in the boardroom of his office. His secretary, Phyllis, tuned into the radio, jotted down the results and slid into the weekly management committee meeting. She pushed the scrap of paper on to his blotter and slipped out. Dad glanced down and read: 'Thatcher, 146; Whitelaw, 79; Howe, 19; Prior, 19 . . .'

'She's done it!' he exclaimed, throwing his hands in the air. His associates, who had deliberately not mentioned a word about the ballot prior to that, jumped up to congratulate him. The entire celebration was over in less than a minute, and then it was business as usual. None of us fully comprehended, on that extraordinary day, the seismic impact Mum's victory would have on our lives.

Having evaded the press outside my exam hall, I walked all the way home in the dusk, via Hyde Park, to find our kitchen looking like a florist's shop. There had been no time for all the congratulatory bouquets to be arranged in vases, so my mother's secretary had sensibly propped them up in buckets and other receptacles while Mum, Dad and Mark went off into the celebratory whirlwind. I tiptoed between the blooms, fled to my friend's house, and watched my mother tell a televised press conference: 'It is like a dream that the next name after Harold Macmillan, Sir Alec Douglas-Home and Ted Heath is Margaret Thatcher.'

I stayed that night in my friend's spare room. When Mum got home, she came to see me. I was half asleep when she knocked on the door. I remember thinking that she instantly looked the part. She was fresh from a party thrown in her honour, and the aura of power about her was almost like a halo. She embraced her new role as if it had always been her destiny. She wished me good luck with my next exam the following day and said goodnight. I went to sleep knowing that nothing was ever going to be the same again.

The next morning, I watched the television news lead with my mother's victory. We were in uncharted territory. On the Tube en route to my exam, I tried to read a fellow passenger's newspaper over his shoulder when I spotted her photograph. Thus began a lifetime of following my mother's movements courtesy of the world's press. He glowered at me and folded it up. 'It's my Mum!' I wanted to say, but then realised he would either think me crazy or terribly rude.

At home, life became even more hectic. A meal in the dining room was out of the question because every inch of the table was filled with thank-you letters laid out alphabetically in House of Commons envelopes like a giant game of Patience. Anyone who passed through our hall was inveigled into licking and sealing a few. All washing-up was postponed because the kitchen was still overflowing with bouquets tied up with oversized blue bows. Mum and her staff dashed in and out of the front door, running the gauntlet of the press photographers who were camped outside our house.

It was the start of what I often describe as the Thatchers' splashdown in the goldfish bowl of public life. From that day on, our personal lives became public property, whether we liked it or not. I even learned, from the pages of a tabloid newspaper, the astonishing news that my father had been married and divorced a few years before he met my mother. The *Daily Mail* sent Lynda Lee-

Potter to interview Mum, and I looked at the photograph of my father's first wife in amazement. 'Don't mention it to your father,' Mum told me when I asked her about it. 'He won't talk about it. It was a wartime thing.'

Everything we did from now on was considered fair game, it seemed, as my mother's campaign to become Britain's first female prime minister began in earnest.

Chapter Five

SPLASHDOWN

THE YEAR 1977 was the halfway mark of my mother's time as leader of Her Majesty's Opposition. Two long years were to pass before the fall of the Labour government headed by James Callaghan, who had replaced Harold Wilson in 1976.

I decided to head Down Under on a working holiday, and my mother asked me if I'd like to accompany her on the way on an official visit to China, Japan and Hong Kong – she said I'd be 'an antidote to too much solemnity'. I jumped at the chance.

In those days the flights to Beijing left from Paris so we had the privilege of overnighting in the British ambassador's residence in the swishest part of the French capital. A magnificent house with a capacious and divine garden, it was once owned by Napoleon Bonaparte's favourite sister.

When we arrived in Beijing we learned that foreign visitors didn't know until the last minute whether they were going to be received by Chairman Hua Guofeng (Mao Zedong had died the previous year). This added a 'tenterhooks' dimension to the daily programme.

An official banquet was arranged for us in the immense and awe-inspiring Great Hall of the People on the west side of Tiananmen Square. It was the hot, dry season, with so much static that Mum had been advised not to wear silk because her dress might cling to her unflatteringly. Even so there was a hitch and, most unusually, my mother was late. She'd had to change at the last minute because her dress was exactly the same colour as the backdrop and she'd have merged into it.

I'd practised my chopsticks technique so as to minimise the risk of table-manners gaffes and chose foods I thought I could manage without committing a chopsticks faux pas. I bypassed slippery numbers like fish bellies, sea slugs and other unidentifiable delicacies. We were served a strong grain spirit called Mao-tai, and it soon became apparent that it was the custom to drink innumerable toasts (which the British journalists took to enthusiastically). Fortunately, women were allowed to sip rather than down what was an almost lethal concoction. While we ate, a Chinese orchestra played a selection of Western favourites, including an interesting arrangement of 'Greensleeves'.

Following Mao's death there was considerable unrest in China, much of it directed at the Soviet Union. Mum embarked on a series of high-level talks with the various political leaders and did her best to smooth the waters.

She also managed to fit in visits to the Great Wall of China and other ancient sites. One day, accompanied by staff from the British embassy and Chinese officials, we were shown around the Summer Palace, a former royal summer residence outside Beijing. This is a highly recommended escape from the hordes of bicyclists and frenzied hooting and congestion in Beijing itself. The guide giving us the history of the palace pointed out an incongruous marble boat permanently marooned on the edge of the lake. One of the embassy staff made his own more recent historical contribution: 'This is exactly the spot where Ted Heath was bundled into a jeep and whisked off for his meeting with Chairman Mao.' It sounded like something out of *Monty Python*, and I swivelled my head around, stared at the boats being rowed around the lake and wondered if one of them would turn into a launch, James Bond-style and cart Mum off into the chairman's presence. We did have a meeting with Chairman Hua but we got there by the more conventional form of transport on these visits: a convoy of limos.

We travelled to Soochow, Hangchow and Shanghai, where we were taken upriver by boat. Mum, always keen to veer off the beaten track, unexpectedly asked to see some British students she knew were enrolled at a university in Shanghai and thus learned that the pristine scene presented to us, complete with copies of

The Economist and *Hansard* in the library, was purely for our benefit.

From China we went on to Tokyo, our last port of call together before I flew to Australia to have a stab at 'jillarooing' on a vast cattle station up in the Northern Territory and try other Outback experiences. There cannot be many gap-year students whose farewell dinner was in the same league as mine. Takeo Fukuda, the prime minister of Japan, gave a banquet in Mum's honour at his official residence. The menu was about as gourmet as it gets and mercifully different from our Chinese banquet. It included *Brioche de Foie Gras Strasbourgeoise*, *Délice de Sole au Chablis* and *Aloyau de Boeuf Rôti*. Later, while downing a foaming beer in the Oz of heat, dust and flies, I sometimes hallucinated about the wine we enjoyed that grand evening in Tokyo: Chevalier Montrachet 1971; Château Mouton Rothschild 1964, and Moët & Chandon, Cuvée Dom Perignon 1969.

One of my mother's official engagements was a visit to a school. I was amused to read in the notes to the itinerary the following sentence: 'Mrs Thatcher may like to know that school hours for the day have been adjusted so as to ensure that her visit is not drowned by the noise of children playing.' 'How considerate' was my reaction; although that was followed by the thought that my mother was so inured to heckling on the campaign trail and the baying racket at Prime Minister's Questions that she might have found happy noise from the playground a novelty and a pleasure.

We also visited the Canon camera plant. I had a personal interest in this because my brother had always ribbed me about being a lousy photographer. 'You ought to get a PHD camera' had been his mantra during our teens. I thought he meant Ph.D and was quite chuffed. In fact he meant 'Press here, dummy.'

The briefing explained that Canon had achieved 'such a lead in world manufacture' because of the quality of its executives on the marketing side and the quality of labour relations. 'The company is forty years old and has never had a strike.' Never mind what it made, this outfit was right up Maggie's street!

Before I left Tokyo I found a rare moment alone with my mother (in the back of an embassy limousine) to wish her luck for the challenges she faced back in the UK. 'I hope it all goes well,' I said, 'and you win the election when it comes.'

Looking out of the window, she showed a flash of self-doubt. 'My great fear is that when the test comes,' she said, 'I might fail.'

Two years later, I was sitting by the telephone in a house I shared in the suburb of Paddington, Sydney. It was early on the morning of 29 March 1979. The sun poured through the windows as I waited, with increasing impatience, for the phone to ring. Twelve thousand miles away, on the floor of the Commons, tension was at a crescendo. Following the famous 'winter of discontent' caused by rising unemployment and industrial disputes, MPs were voting on a motion of no confidence which the opposition had tabled against Jim Callaghan's Labour government.

Having personally written to scores of MPs, urging them to attend the vote and help bring the government down, my mother made a speech which electrified the House. The expectation was palpable as MPs began to file into the division lobbies to vote. My father was sitting in the Chamber in a box next to Maggie Atkins, wife of the chief whip, Humphrey Atkins, when the tellers (the MPs who count the votes) walked forward at around 10.30 p.m. to declare the result: Ayes, 311; Noes, 310. Jim Callaghan had lost by a single vote.

Dad threw his arms in the air in a gesture of jubilation and exclaimed, 'Done it!' as if celebrating a try at Twickenham. This was unacceptable conduct for a non-Member and he was quietly and justifiably reprimanded by a serjeant-at-arms. In the light of the vote, Jim Callaghan was obliged to advise the Queen that he would be calling a general election in a few months' time.

My phone managed just one ring before I seized it. Alison Ward, my mother's secretary, squawked ecstatically down the line, her voice bouncing off the inter-continental telephonic gadgets between the leader of the opposition's office in Westminster and my house on the shores of Sydney Harbour.

'Your mother wants to tell you herself,' Alison cried, 'but we won!'

It was thrilling news, but I wanted more detail and the line wasn't good.

'By how many?' I asked.

'One,' she replied.

I thought Alison was repeating 'won'. Eventually I realised what she was saying and blurted: 'One? That's not many.'

By now, Mum was on the line and she heard me. She was her usual pragmatic self. 'We didn't need many,' she reminded me.

I asked when the general election was likely to be, and offered my hearty congratulations. Always security-conscious, she rarely replied directly to any questions of political or national importance, and remained vague.

Once I'd replaced the receiver, I thought that for me, the day would be business as usual – a bus ride to my office and several hours writing features. Throughout the day, though, I was constantly reminded of events back home, as congratulatory phone calls flooded in.

The polls looked promising and the general enthusiasm fuelled the belief that my mother was on the way to becoming Britain's first female prime minister. As her daughter, even though I was twelve thousand miles away I was soon caught up in the media whirlwind. About ten o'clock that night, after what had been a busy and exciting day, a photographer turned up at my home to take a photo of me and my housemates. I hurriedly tidied up, painfully aware that, once again, my personal life was about to come under intense scrutiny.

After he left, my mind rewound to the previous autumn when we'd been waiting for what we hoped would be an announcement of the next election. It was Thursday, 7 September, and my mother was in Birmingham. Political speculation predicted that in his prime ministerial broadcast that evening Jim Callaghan would announce that he was going to the country. Mum, however, knew differently. She had received an advance call from Number Ten to let her know, in confidence, that Callaghan's broadcast would announce that there wasn't going to be an election after all. She must have been hugely deflated after all the hype, but had to carry on for the rest of the day accepting numerous 'Good luck, Maggie' messages, unable to give anything away until the news became public knowledge.

Back in Sydney, I scoured the archives of the reference library of the *Sydney Morning Herald* in search of an appropriate quotation to put in an international telegram to Mum. I eventually found a quote from a play by the Jacobean tragedian John Ford: 'Delay in vengeance gives a heavier blow.' I thought it conveyed the right note. I added, 'Callaghan's procrastination will be your landslide majority,' and sent the wire off straight away. To this day I don't know if she received it, or if she twigged that the quotation came from one of the most controversial plays in English literature, *'Tis Pity She's a Whore*.

On the night of the successful no-confidence vote six months later my mother telephoned Tim (later Lord) Bell, head of Saatchi & Saatchi, who handled Tory party advertising and had masterminded its brilliant campaign under the slogan 'Labour Isn't Working'. She wanted to glean his reaction and that of Gordon Reece, her press adviser, political strategist and so-called 'image builder', who had done everything from arranging voice lessons for her to making her abandon her trademark hats.

When the news came in, Tim and Gordon had taken the only sensible option when the unexpected happens in politics: they had repaired to the nearest licensed premises. Tim was fast asleep by the time Mum called. As he sat up and began talking to her as soberly as he could about the political implications of Callaghan's announcement, he cast his eyes around his home, which seemed unusually untidy. Halfway through the conversation, he suddenly exclaimed, 'My God! I've been burgled.' That fact had earlier escaped him in the drama and drink of the evening.

Despite the fact that I was twelve thousand miles away, Mum kept me informed as best she could of all the preparations for the election campaign – she always amazed me with her ability to switch from major international or political matters to minute domestic details. But I felt very far away – and regretted it – when Airey Neave, my mother's campaign manager, head of her private office and former shadow secretary of state for Northern Ireland, was killed by an INLA car bomb as he left the House of Commons car park.

I read Mum's moving tributes to him in the newspapers the following day. 'He was one of freedom's warriors,' she said, fighting back the tears, 'courageous, staunch, true. He lived for his beliefs and now he has died for them.' My brother once said that, of all the trials and tribulations Mum had to face in her long political career, losing Airey Neave was the hardest for her to bear.

She said she felt 'like a puppet whose strings had been cut'. What was described at the time as 'the scourge of terrorism' was at its height in Britain then, with the IRA's assassination of Lord Mountbatten and members of his family later that year and the murders of eighteen British soldiers at Warrenpoint. Within a year there would also be the Iranian embassy siege in London.

Mum's letters to me in Australia, which usually began: 'Dear Carol Jane' revealed her emotions at that time of the Mountbatten and Warrenpoint murders:

The terrible events of last Monday still dominate one's feelings and the news. We feel equally strongly about the Mountbatten family murders and the ... British soldiers killed. I decided to go to Ulster last Wednesday to demonstrate togetherness with the people and concern for our soldiers. Three of those killed in the army were only eighteen – others nineteen and twenty. It was an appalling waste of young life. I visited the hospital where some of the injured were being treated. I spoke to one policeman who had lost both a leg and an arm in an IRA radio remote-controlled explosion. He was remarkable. He only wanted to get back into the police force. I did a walkabout in the shopping centre [in Belfast]. The people were marvellous – and they were so glad to see me there and so anxious to express their horror and concern and begged one to 'do something' to stop it. The question is precisely what. So long as there is a safe haven south of the border for terrorists we shall not be able to get on top of the situation. In the afternoon I flew by helicopter down to the border areas and went to the military post from which our boys were lost. As I came away one of the privates said to me, 'Thank you for coming, at least someone cares.'

Despite the devastating loss of Airey Neave – indeed, because of it – the campaign had to go on. My mother said it was 'what Airey would have wanted'. In the starting-blocks, poised for the off, she developed a manic determination to convert every floating voter in every marginal to the cause. Still, she found time on her hands. Ronnie Millar, who used to 'Ronnify' some of Ma's speeches, remembered in his book *A View from the Wings* that the lack of action was anything but satisfactory.

Until the campaign proper got under way, there was nothing to do but wait. Doing nothing is something that Margaret Thatcher has always been extremely bad at. She fretted restlessly, finding work for idle hands, dictating letters that were not necessary, inventing problems that didn't exist and generally driving her devoted secretaries to distraction. It was like waiting for D-Day.

The woman who might, within weeks, become Britain's first female prime minister, had to be found something other than twiddling her thumbs to do. Ronnie was therefore instructed to organise some theatre excursions. Mum and Dad were duly despatched to see the Two Ronnies, of whom she had become a fan after watching them on television (something she rarely, if ever, found time to do). These theatre outings continued throughout the Number Ten years and sometimes involved the whole family. As the years went by, Ronnie Millar and I used to take bets on which of my parents would fall asleep first after the curtain went up.

I flew home to join the campaign halfway through, standing alongside Mum and Dad in the front yard of their home in Flood Street for an impromptu photo call; Mark was away on a business trip at the time. The photograph appeared in several newspapers the following day, some with the headline 'Carol Joins Maggie's Campaign'. In fact, they couldn't have been further from the truth. Mum's campaign team had sensibly decided that, as I hadn't even read the Conservative Party manifesto, I should be kept well away from voters. Fortunately, I didn't blow anything with my remark: 'I think Mum is doing very well.' The then treasurer of the Tory party, Alistair McAlpine, captured the spirit of the times in his book, *Once a Jolly Bagman*: 'Working in Central Office during that election was a lot of fun – working anywhere is a lot of fun when you are winning.'

On polling day, 4 May 1979, the headlines were largely positive. 'Maggie Aims for 250!' trumpeted the *Daily Express*, before explaining, 'This morning's magic figure for Mrs Margaret

Thatcher and the Tories is two hundred and fifty. That is the number of seats they'll have to win overnight to have a chance of forming a majority government.'

On polling day Mum, Dad, Mark and I all voted at nine o'clock in the morning and then toured polling stations in Finchley. We returned home to Flood Street in the early evening. Those were really fraught hours. It was like waiting for the result of an exam. My mother was a total fidget, unable to sit still for more than a few seconds, and eventually took to clearing out drawers and disposing of piles of paper in her office, ripping them into confetti-sized pieces. It was as if being a one-woman shredding machine calmed her nerves.

By the time we got to Barnet town hall for the count, shortly before midnight, an ITN exit poll was encouragingly predicting an overall Conservative majority of sixty-three (in fact, it ended up being forty-four). When victory was confirmed, no one had a broader grin than Dad. After four years in opposition, wondering if Mum would ever make it to Number Ten, the reality finally hit home. It was actually happening – and to us!

In Conservative Central Office the morning after, we waited for the call summoning my mother to Buckingham Palace to see the Queen. Even this had its comical moments. My mother's personal assistant and close confidante, Crawfie (Cynthia Crawford), had already left to go to Number Ten with her staff, laden with typewriters, files and other office paraphernalia. Before leaving, they posed for a photograph, wearing tops emblazoned with the slogan 'I Thought On the Rocks Was a Drink Until I Discovered the Labour Government'.

Every time the phone rang, we jumped in anticipation. Caroline Stephens, my mother's diary secretary, always answered. 'Wrong number,' she informed us, so we relaxed. Except, of course, Mum, who was in the habit of going unnecessarily overboard about imagined – and highly unlikely – obstacles. This time her predicament was: what if she bumped into Jim Callaghan as he went to the Palace to hand in his seals of office, just as she arrived to be asked to form a government?

'It would be embarrassing,' she said. 'I wouldn't want him to think I'm rubbing it in.'

I was astounded. She'd won the election only a few hours earlier; she hadn't even got the job yet; and here she was feeling sorry for the guy she'd been trying to oust from Number Ten for the last three years.

Dad brought some much-needed reality to the situation by reminding her, 'Buck House has been doing this for years. I imagine they know the form by now.'

Phew, I thought. Common sense at last.

Caroline reappeared, having answered the telephone once more.

'Sir Philip Moore from the Palace,' she announced. My mother left to take the call in an adjacent office and then returned.

'We're off,' she said, in that urgent tone we knew so well.

Dad calmly pointed out that, with no traffic lights to stop

at and police outriders to accompany her, at this rate they'd be early. I added that doing endless circuits of Victoria Monument would look a bit daft, while kerb-crawling might not give the right impression for the country's first female prime minister.

Actually, I half blame Alison for Mum's attitude to punctuality. Alison was a fully paid-up member of what we called Mum's 'Stopwatch Club'. One of her mantras was, 'You might have a puncture on the way. You could even have two!'

My father – in the long-gone days when he and Mum travelled by rail – used to claim that she didn't just want to catch a train, she wanted to be on the platform to welcome it in. Even years into their sojourn at Number Ten, Mum and Dad's ideas of timing never quite matched. There would be a regular sitting-room scene in the flat prior to a 7.30 p.m. scheduled departure:

7.15: Mum in long dress, ready to go, speech in one hand, handbag in the other. She asks me, 'Does DT know we're leaving at 7.30 p.m.?'
'Yes, Mum, I'm sure he does.'
7.25: Dad appears and pours himself a gin and tonic, while Mum reminds him of their departure time.
'I know,' he says, polishing off his drink.

I often wondered why, after thirty-odd years of marriage, she hadn't clicked that he always turned up five, not fifteen, minutes before the off, and could down a gin in one. Not to mention the fact that as he was being dragged, uncomplaining, to yet another political dinner, he surely deserved some fortification first.

Needless to say, on the day Mum had to go to the Palace, she left so early that the driver virtually had to crawl along The Mall. This was to be the last time for many years that she sat in the back of the leader of the opposition's car. Once she left the Palace, she would step into Jim Callaghan's old vehicle, and he into hers. It was all arranged seamlessly.

As the car 'trod water', Dad sat beside her staring out into leafy St James's Park. He confided to me later that his mind was racing. 'I suddenly started to worry about what I was going to be doing while Margaret was seeing the Queen,' he said. He needn't have worried. There was, of course, a protocol for spouses in just that situation, and he was whisked off to a private drawing room to enjoy a nice cup of tea with two of the Queen's staff. (Years later, at a lunch aboard QE2, I met one of the Queen's ladies-in-waiting who had been on duty that day. She told me that Dad had been offered a cup of tea but, characteristically, had opted for a gin and tonic!)

When the formalities were over, the new prime minister stepped into her new vehicle and a police motorcycle escort swept them towards Downing Street. Dad noticed that the guards saluted Mum on the way out, which they hadn't done in the way in.

Mark and I went on ahead in a taxi and were ushered into the hall at Number Ten. The mustard-coloured carpet was barely visible beneath the feet of the hordes of staff lined up to receive the new prime minister. Dad and Mark took up positions to greet Mum on the doorstep 'like a couple of well-trained guards', according to one newspaper, while I stood at the back, totally overawed, telling myself, 'Don't do anything wrong, don't embarrass anyone.'

Mum stood on the steps for the world's press and recited the prayer of St Francis of Assisi:

> Where there is discord, may we bring harmony.
> Where there is error, may we bring truth.
> Where there is doubt, may we bring faith.
> Where there is despair, may we bring hope.

Then, deeply moved by the moment, she turned and walked through the door into Number Ten to be greeted by a spontaneous burst of applause. Having been formally introduced to her staff of around eighty (compared to four hundred in the White House and five hundred in the German Chancellery), she was scooped up by her political team and led deeper into the building for strategy meetings and further introductions. She would remain there until much later that night, sharing a Chinese takeaway with her team in the rather grand setting of the State Dining Room.

Dad, Mark and I were left, rather surplus to requirements, standing in the hallway. My parents wouldn't be able to move in for another month. Someone told us that an official car would take us back to Flood Street. Turning to say goodbye, the last we saw of Mum was her perfect blonde hair and her Tory-blue suit disappearing along the corridors of power at a purposeful pace.

Chapter Six

BRAND-NEW BOWL

FOR ELEVEN AND a half years my parents' home was 10 Downing Street, London SW1 1AA – among the top political addresses in the world.

I yo-yoed in and out frequently, sometimes popping in on my way to work in order to say hello to my mother while she was having her hair done, at other times dropping in late at night on the way home from the West End when she might have a moment to look up from her red boxes for an updating chat.

Sometimes I felt like an ordinary Londoner as I walked from Westminster Tube station, glancing up at Big Ben – always one of my favourite London landmarks – along Whitehall then turning left into a sunless side-street which runs down to St James's Park.

Apart from the policeman on the doorstep, and the fact that there were no keys to the shiny front door because it was manned twenty-four hours a day by a doorman, Number Ten was nothing jaw-dropping. In the days when the public could still wander up the street, the policeman used to lend his helmet for the on-the-doorstep snaps. Once I heard an earnest American, who looked up after checking his guidebook, ask the copper, 'Does Sherlock Holmes really live here?' Wrong celeb, pal, I was tempted to correct him, but the policeman got in first – much more diplomatically. On another occasion, a couple were admiring the exterior of the Foreign Office in Downing Street, with its magnificent façade and lofty wrought-iron gates which lead to a capacious quadrangle of considerable grandeur. 'Is this where the prime minister lives?' they asked me.

'No,' I replied, willing to play impromptu tour leader. 'The Prime Minister lives in Number Ten on the other side of the street – behind you.'

They spun round, gawped, and exclaimed, 'Wow! That little townhouse?'

The image and reality of calling Number Ten home are a spectrum apart. The 1981 James Bond film *For Your Eyes Only* featured Janet Brown, a Scottish comedienne, who did a mean Maggie impersonation, and John Wells as my parents in a little cameo scene supposedly set in the kitchen in Downing Street. How those of us who used the real galley kitchen in the private flat drooled over the movie version with its shiny, showroom-polished aura, loaded with mod cons and gadgets and so well stocked . . . The real thing was Spartan and very out-of-date, with no guarantee of hot water out of the taps at washing-up time. Yet, judging by the questions I was constantly asked, many people were under the misapprehension that the prime minister's life was illuminated by chandeliers, with hot-and-cold running footmen catering to her every whim.

When it came to official entertaining everything was very smooth and highly efficient. Upstairs in the private flat it was rather more DIY. When my mother invited someone for drinks I would often open our fridge to find that the ice-trays hadn't been filled and have to belt down to the catering kitchen next to the State Dining Room on the floor below and help myself from the ice-machine there. I then sprinted back up the stairs, hoping no one would notice the ultra-kitsch ice-bucket my mother had picked up at a bring-and-buy stall at one of the fêtes in her constituency.

Besides being one of the most famous addresses in the world, Number Ten is the ultimate tied cottage that goes with the job of being prime minister. But, however long you are there, the most prevalent thought you have is the fact that it is only a temporary home. There is one main daily reminder: the long line of portraits showcasing all the previous prime ministers, dating back to Walpole who was the first to live there.

The daughter of a previous prime minister, Lady Violet Bonham Carter, wrote of Number Ten: 'If walls of brick and stone can hold, for all time, some intangible deposit of the great events which once took place within their span, no human dwelling should have a richer heritage than Number Ten Downing Street. It is a "house of history" in which the past is a living presence not to be put by.'

It is actually much bigger than you would think. The prime minister's private flat was converted out of the attic and overlooked Horse Guards Parade at the back. In estate-agent-speak, it has five or six bedrooms. They, like the kitchen and the bathrooms, were very old-fashioned, unimaginatively furnished and anything but state-of-the-art. Even though Number Ten is at the heart of the nation's political life, up in the flat you can, rather incongruously, feel wholly isolated from the political machinations and crises playing out a floor or two below.

In my mother's time, it was handy to keep your shock absorbers well primed. There was always a buzz once you stepped through the front door, crossed the black-and-white floor of the entrance hall and made your way along the carpeted corridor that connects the front, Downing Street part of the building to the back, which overlooks the garden and then Horse Guards Parade.

Living there, you could always fall back on the excuse that you were only the tenant or lodger. I once had a party in one of the first-floor reception rooms overlooking Horse Guards Parade so that the guests could watch a floodlit performance of Beating the Retreat. This is a military ceremony with massed bands, drummers and trumpeters; and under floodlights, against the backdrop of the night descending on St James's Park, it is both a magical and an impressive display.

One guest took her eyes off the spectacle to inform me disapprovingly, 'Your net curtains need a good wash.'

'Oh, they're the government's not ours.' I felt like the golf caddie who said, 'We were doing really well until he hit a bad shot.'

There certainly were occasions when I felt the hostility of the voters and it was abundantly clear that the object of their wrath was my mother. Most often it was when demonstrations convened in Trafalgar Square and then marched down Whitehall. The noisy, aggressive chants of 'Maggie, Maggie, Maggie, Out Out Out' left no one in Number Ten in any doubt that they were on the wrong side of the barricades. I don't think I ever expected to be lynched by the mob, but it was unsettling and very much the flipside of electoral glory.

My father had a calming influence during dramas. 'Let's get relaxed,' he would beseech the prime minister's staff, and then pour stiff gins for those looking in need of his favourite tipple.

Flicking through my father's black Lett's Slim Pocket Planner for 1979, there are only occasional clues that he was married to the prime minister and lived at this famous address:

4 June: Move to Number Ten

12 June: State Banquet Buck Ho

16 June: Trooping (the Colour)

10 July: [as if still pinching himself]: Own Cocktails. Me

The removal vans arrived early at Flood Street on 4 June, loaded up with tea-chests and packing crates, which were filled and taken to Number Ten. Once inside the famous shiny black door, the removal men made their way up the main staircase and then through a rabbit warren of passageways, to the second-floor self-contained flat that was Mum and Dad's new home. There were very few large items, because of the lack of space and because the flat was already plainly furnished with regulation government-issue.

My mother always enjoyed 'living over the shop', it suited her never-off-duty attitude. The floor plan of the apartment resembles an extended railway carriage, with the main bedroom on the left (with two single beds pushed together), and an en suite bathroom, which doubled as a hairdressers most mornings. Further along the hallway is a drawing room which overlooks Horse Guards Parade, then another bedroom and dressing room for guests. Along the corridor, on the right, is a laundry with washing machine, freezer and fridge, a bedroom which Mark snaffled, and another which Dad used for his office. Up three steps is a small guest room which I used whenever I stayed there. At the end of the passageway, Joy Robilliard, Mum's constituency secretary, who used to work for Airey Neave, set up her office. At the back of the flat, down several steps, are a galley kitchen and an unimposing dining room, into which we could just squash eight.

Government regulations state that the incumbent prime minister has to pay a service charge and make their own domestic arrangements. Mum took Mossie, our cleaning lady from Flood Street, with her and hired another, called Edwina, but she decreed that no cook or housekeeper could cope with the long and irregular hours, so she wouldn't hire one. Joy therefore became general dogsbody – shopping for food, organising the flat and fielding telephone calls as well as performing her own considerable duties. Without Joy, none of the rest of us would ever have kept up to date with Mum's schedule. Downstairs was managed entirely separately. Mum and Dad were sometimes woken early in the morning by the sound of vacuuming down below, and cushions being plumped noisily.

In the flat, entertaining was especially haphazard. People would arrive for a drink and be surprised to find the new prime minister alone in the flat, dashing around trying to coordinate glasses, lemon, gin and tonic. Colleagues and speechwriters who stayed late enough to join her for supper would watch, amazed, as Mum flitted between the latest passage of a speech to the stove to watch something on the boil; often, she reheated leftovers brought back from Chequers. Eventually, she had the caterer from downstairs make her a series of 'shove in the oven and heat up' dishes for the freezer – usually lasagne or shepherd's pie. In fact, lasagne became such a staple that visitors groaned at the sight of it.

Back in Australia, and feeling very far away, I longed to hear about life at Number Ten, and my parents' other experiences, like going to Balmoral that first September after she was elected. I have no idea how generous the Royal Household is when it comes to the allocation of notepaper in the guest suites at the Scottish royal residence, but it must have been pretty good as, in-between admiring views of the heather-clad hills, my mother found time to pen me eight heavy pages of news, each with a beautiful red crest on the top. The cost of postage must have been considerably higher than the usual blue airmail letters my political pen pal sent me (and her secretary addressed for her) from the House of Commons post office.

We are here on the customary weekend for the Prime Minister – a very nice custom, she began. After telling me her political movements that week, she gave me a Maggie-tour of Balmoral which, while lacking in the detail I might have liked, like the decor, left me feeling I could almost smell the damp heather:

Then a drive around the estate, which is some forty thousand acres of beautiful but not very fertile land. They have some sheep and cattle but no arable crops. The cost of keeping the estate going must be enormous. After tea we came to the castle where we are staying. There are several of the young Royals staying – Prince Edward and Princess Margaret's two children – and Prince Andrew comes today (Sunday).

Today, a walk before church, then the service, and I

understand another drive to a different part of the estate this afternoon. We leave this evening, and we are taking the three young Royals back to London with us because they have to return to school tomorrow.

Of all the letters that arrived during that time, my favourite was a sequence which arrived helpfully numbered One to Four because, if you have acquired a chemistry degree at Oxford, followed by a spell as a barrister then prime minister, you wouldn't like your daughter to read your news in the wrong order!

It was wonderful to talk to you on Sunday . . . and hear how things are going with you . . . Parliament rose at the end of last week after a pretty hectic last few days. The previous week we had the censure debate, which went well for us. Then two days later I gave my annual talk to the 1922 Committee . . .

After several pages on the teachers' arbitration award, some chat about her difficult parliamentary week, and her concerns about how to make British industries competitive with that of other nations, air letter Number Four began: 'Enough of politics for the time being!' She gave me details of their impending Swiss holiday, which, she said, would have a high work content and a low leisure one, with dinners for Swiss bankers and businessmen and a trip to the embassy in Berne, and then got onto the subject of Number Ten.

I knew Mum thought the décor was shabby, but spending government money was out of the question, so she eventually had the hideous green flock wallpaper in her office changed at her own expense. What a contrast to the furore over the £650,000 Lord Irvine spent almost twenty years later on hand-printed designer wallpaper and other adornments for the lord chancellor's apartment in the House of Lords. He justified his expenditure to the Commons Public Administration Committee as 'a noble cause'.

My mother was very pragmatic and economical, and, harnessing the common sense acquired as a grocer's daughter, to make her new home more comfortable she raided other government grace and favour flats. Obviously satisfied with the results, she wrote me a long letter about it:

Hearing that we had three flats in Admiralty House that are not used, [I] went on a tour of inspection. As a result, I decided that some of the poor furniture from the flat could go there to collect dust, and some of their nicer furniture could come here to be used. Our sitting room and the downstairs study have now been transformed. We have two lovely large settees, beautifully covered, three velvet chairs, a small elegant desk, a genuine chiffonier – the other was repro – and a lovely side table. Downstairs, the faded suite has gone and we have an oyster colour settee and two chairs in its place. The old heavy mahogany chairs have gone – to be replaced by six yellow silk chairs. We have also brought from Admiralty House about ten spare table lamps and a lovely display cabinet. So without spending any money we have improved the place no end. We all helped in the removals and everyone enjoyed themselves . . .

There was no need for any such wily schemes at Chequers, an elegant house which is the epitome of grandeur. My father perfectly described what residences meant to prime ministers and their families. 'Chequers: that was really why you got the job.'

As the beneficiary of endless hospitality at both Downing Street and Chequers between 1979 and 1990, especially after I returned from Australia in 1981, I was in a very fortunate position. I became the perpetual reserve if a dinner guest dropped out at the last minute. Whenever the call came to fill the empty chair, it always reminded me of the split life I led. As an impecunious freelance journalist, travel writer and radio reporter suddenly in receipt of a last-minute invitation to Number Ten (even if it was via my Mum), I would go into a blind panic, searching through my scruffy wardrobe for something which wouldn't be too embarrassing to show up in. This usually meant sprinting to the cleaners for their same-day service, or sewing on some buttons with one of the mini sewing kits I had acquired from some posh hotel.

More often than not, I also had to dash out and buy a new pair of tights, and polish a pair of shoes with some potion guaranteed to give them instant shine, before rushing to Whitehall in my antiquated second-hand car (British, of course).

Having seen the state of my trusty (sometimes not so trusty) lime-green Ford Fiesta, and knowing that I frequently had to recruit passers-by to push-start it, the powers-that-be decreed that I should park on Horse Guards Parade. Mark, who had a much more up-market, state-of-the-art Lotus was permitted to park in Downing Street.

By far the grandest and most memorable of my 'free-meals-from-Mum's-job' was a dinner in 1985 to celebrate the two hundred and fiftieth anniversary of the house being the official home of the prime minister. The Queen and the Duke of Edinburgh were among the guests, as were all living former prime ministers and a direct descendant of every incumbent since Asquith. As I ran my eye over the guest list, I marvelled at the memories daughters of past prime ministers must have of their time in Number Ten: Lady Olwen Carey Evans, daughter of Lloyd George; Lady Soames, daughter of Winston Churchill; Mrs Sheila Lockhead (Ramsay MacDonald), and Mrs Dorothy Lloyd (Neville Chamberlain). Fleetingly, I wondered how I would look back when Mum was no longer PM.

I had already been to Wales to interview ninety-three-year-old Lady Olwen for a news feature. She was a real old hand at Downing Street, having lived in both Number Ten and Number Eleven, and she had a fund of lively and entertaining anecdotes. She told me that after she had finished a cooking course her father, Lloyd George, who was then PM, insisted on finding out for himself if the course had been value for money. He instructed her to cook a meal to be served in Number Ten's dining room. The kitchen staff were not allowed to assist. She did her best but knew the meat looked slightly rare as it was taken up to the prime minister and his guests.

When she joined them for coffee later, Lloyd George marked his daughter's culinary efforts in verse: 'Now the meal is over, we sigh with longing grief/For the mealie tatties and the bloody beef.' After Lady Olwen returned from a language course in France, she faced another paternal prime ministerial test: never mind the official interpreter, would she translate for her father during his meeting with the French munitions minister? She recalled convincing her father that, if not yet bilingual, she had been a conscientious student. That was until the discussion got a bit technical and 'barbed wire entanglements' had to be negotiated. These fortifications, unsurprisingly, weren't on her vocabulary list and completely stumped her.

Originally, I wasn't invited to this historic anniversary dinner but had managed to inveigle myself an invitation to the pre-dinner drinks. Sadly, there seemed little chance that any of the guests would cancel; after all, it was only the third time in the Queen's reign that she had dined at Number Ten. The first had been in 1955, on the eve of Winston Churchill's resignation, and the second in 1976 when Harold Wilson left office. Arriving at Number Ten, I met one of the caterers, who asked whether I was in on the dinner.

'No, alas,' I replied, 'just the drinks.'

'Pity,' he said. 'Just a whiff of the wine is fantastic.'

As I raced up the Grand Staircase, past all the portraits of former prime ministers, to change, my mother's secretary greeted me with the terrific news that the wife of David Steel – then leader of the Liberal Party – had fallen victim to the wintry December weather and couldn't make it down from Scotland. I was in!

To this day, I remember the cover of the menu. It was a beautiful watercolour of Downing Street which exuded a remarkable air of peace and tranquillity. You'd never guess that the front door was the entrance and exit of so many political dramas over the last two and a half centuries. Just reading what we were going to eat and drink made my mouth water. I'd already been tipped off about the quality of the wine, of course, and it didn't disappoint. It included Château Latour 1955, Krug 1964, Quinta do Noval 1931 and Hine 1906. The food was equally impressive:

Game Consommé with Paprika Straws
Paupiettes of Sole and Salmon with Moselle Sauce
Fillets of Veal and Beef with Wild Mushrooms and Béarnaise Sauce
French Beans with Tomato
Vichy Carrots
Parisienne Potatoes
Pineapple and Mango Romanoff with Palmier Biscuits
Coffee

I enjoyed every mouthful.

My father once said that he really twigged he was the husband of the prime minister when he accompanied her on an official visit to see the troops in Northern Ireland. The top military brass were waiting at the bottom of the aircraft's steps to welcome them. The PM left the aircraft first, followed by Dad. As he, too, was saluted by a man with scrambled egg on his epaulettes, his reaction was: 'By God! I've arrived.'

My own 'Can this really be happening to me?' moment was at that remarkable anniversary dinner, sipping the most superb wine I was ever likely to taste. I had to pinch myself to convince myself that I was really there, as the Scots Guards added to the surreal atmosphere with a programme of music which included excerpts from Mozart's *Eine Kleine Nachtmusik* and compositions by Schubert, Haydn and Handel. Round the table, which was topped with massive gold candelabra and glorious arrangements of pink carnations and orchids, was a cast straight out of the history books; people who had stamped their mark on the story of our country. The Queen made a delightful speech. She quipped that, by this stage in her father's reign, he'd been a guest at Number Ten far more often. 'I was beginning to wonder what I'd done wrong!'

Afterwards, over coffee in the Pillared Room, I chatted to Harold and Mary Wilson. In a room full of women wearing brand-new evening dresses, Mrs Wilson took justifiable pride in wearing the same dress she'd worn the last time the Queen came to dinner at Number Ten, in 1976.

Many of the elderly guests had spent some of their childhood in the house, and became misty-eyed as the memories came flooding back. Dorothy Chamberlain had attended her father's dinner for King George VI and Queen Elizabeth in 1939. 'It was very formal – white tie and decorations and lots of tiaras. The King and Queen had to have their own chairs. Two beautiful red velvet ones were brought over from Buckingham Palace, and because the Queen was so small there was a matching footstool for her to rest her tiny legs on.'

I wondered idly if any of the guests realised that the chairs they were sitting on were, in fact, rejects. They had once been in the British embassy in Rio de Janeiro but when Brazil's purpose-built capital, Brasilia, was completed, and a new embassy opened there, the Adam chairs were deemed past it and wound up in the State Dining Room in Number Ten.

Another early official dinner I remember clearly was one held nine months earlier in honour of President Hosni Mubarak of Egypt. Dad and I used to get an advance seating plan and a guest list which gave us a few clues to who the other guests were and why they were there. The Mubarak one had all the usual suspects: the Egyptian presidential delegation and members of Her Majesty's Government, as well as guests from the Conservative, Liberal and Labour parties and from the House of Lords. Then there were businessmen with links to Egypt, including Mohamed Fayed, who had recently purchased Harrods, where I had once worked. Could anyone have peered into a crystal ball and foreseen how much more we would be hearing of that man over the coming years?

The snakes and ladders of the guest lists and seating plans

always rather intrigued me. Scanning the list for the Egyptian dinner, I wondered if I'd have to discuss sewage treatment with the gentleman to my right, who was involved in putting together a waste-water scheme in Cairo. Or might I learn about watering the desert, courtesy of the gent on my left, the managing director of a firm ('small but very active', the blurb said) supplying irrigation to the Arab Republic of Egypt? The evening was made for me by the fact that I was just seven seats away from the very good-looking Omar Sharif, who played Sherif Ali ibn el-Kharish in *Lawrence of Arabia* and the title role in one of my all-time favourite films, *Dr Zhivago*.

Dad, of course, sat next to President Mubarak's wife, who was part-Welsh. I am sure he sneaked an opportunity to discuss epic rugby football matches at Cardiff Arms Park. If not, he had the great Welsh baritone Sir Geraint Evans and his wife on the other side, and Dad wasn't too bad on opera, so I was relieved on his behalf. A naturally shy man, he often kept a card of emergency subjects in his pocket to resort to when chat lines to first ladies ran out.

Once, seated next to the wife of an African leader, who was attired splendidly in the ceremonial dress of her homeland, he had to resort to enquiring of this non-English speaker whether she was enjoying her lunch. 'Likey soupy?' he tried. It was phrase book stuff! Dad was always so gallant – a trait of his generation. He once volunteered that the reason he had always got on with Nancy (Reagan) and Raisa (Gorbachev) was because he wasn't trying to get off with them.

Both my parents adored entertaining at Chequers. Sometimes, in his favourite London restaurants, he could be heard asking friends on another table: 'When are you coming down to the ranch?' If he knew someone was about to visit and he saw them during the week, he'd insist that if they arrived early they mustn't park in the lay-by in the lane (a popular ruse) but come straight in, because the PM didn't like him getting stuck into the gin until the first guests had arrived. Once they all had their drinks in hand, Dad delighted in the role of tour guide, showing guests around.

The first time I visited, Mark accompanied me and we got hopelessly lost. I did the navigating and Mark, who had a passion for motor sports, drove like a maniac (as always) and we only just made it for dinner. Victory Drive, the entrance, which is gun-barrel straight and lined with beech trees gifted by Churchill, sweeps up to the red-brick and grey-stone Tudor building. I have often been asked to describe Chequers. I liken it to a boutique hotel in the heart of the English countryside. By stately home standards it is modest, with only ten bedrooms, but, as my mother wrote in her memoirs, 'I do not think anyone has stayed long at Chequers without falling in love with it.' She adored the place as much as Dad and I did.

There has been a house on the site of Chequers since the twelfth century, although the current one dates from the sixteenth. It served as a hospital and convalescent home for soldiers in the First World War and was then gifted to the nation, along with a thousand acres, by Lord Lee of Fareham; it has been the prime minister's official country residence since 1921. A stained-glass window in the Long Gallery reads, '*This house of peace and ancient memories was given to England as a thank-offering for her deliverance in the Great War, 1914–1918, and as a place of rest and recreation for her Prime Ministers for ever.*'

The highlight of the building is the Great Hall, once an open courtyard, but now with a colossally high ceiling and dramatic theatre-style curtain all along one side. My mother met us there the first time Mark and I arrived and gave us the grand tour. The Hall is of colossal height, with a theatre stage-length curtain on one side and an ornate carved wooden gallery running along the first floor of another. My favourite memory is of Dad's seventieth birthday in May 1985, when we set up round tables in the Great Hall and guests helped themselves to an enormous buffet laid out in the adjacent room. Mum bustled around, constantly reminding everyone, 'It's Denis's party.' There were loads of his old rugby pals, and the champagne flowed. Mum kept topping up their plates, doling out great dollops of curry and turkey, ribs and vegetables. When the party was over I asked to keep the empty Salmanazer (which holds nine litres) as a souvenir. This slightly surprised the staff, who weren't accustomed to a member of the PM's family asking to keep the empties!

The dining room at Chequers is particularly handsome, with a wall of windows looking south over the sunken rose garden and beyond, all the way down Victory Drive to the main gates. It is panelled, and has a table big enough for around twenty guests and a small, round table in the bay window – the latter was the one preferred by my parents, and we always used it as a family.

On Sunday mornings we came down to breakfast to find all the newspapers laid out on the sideboard. If the prime minister and the government were having a particularly bad press, there was an almost firing-line-like atmosphere as we read, fumed and commented on leader writers' and journalists' opinions while tucking into toast and marmalade, followed by the usual works. I used to try to focus on the cartoons rather than the stories, but it was Dad who minded his wife being 'shot at' most of all, shouting 'Rubbish!' from behind the pages. My mother often didn't read the papers at all because she didn't want the distraction.

I bet few of the guests invited to Chequers on 16 December 1984 had any inkling of the role that meal of sole in shrimp sauce, fillet of beef, and oranges in caramel would have on changing the world. The lunch was in honour of the visit to the United Kingdom by a delegation from the USSR Supreme Soviet, led by Mr M. S. Gorbachev 'Member of the Politburo and Secretary of the General Committee of the CPSU and Chairman of the Foreign Affairs Commission of the Council of the Union of the USSR Supreme Soviet', accompanied by Mrs R. M. Gorbachev.

'It was extraordinary,' Dad told me. 'At the time one doesn't say that it was history in the making, but I realised that this was something pretty special.' My mother's comment was equally memorable. 'This is a man I can do business with,' she said. 'Gorby', as he was soon dubbed, was on the map. Three months later he succeeded Konstantin Chernenko as Soviet leader.

Denis showed Mrs Gorbachev the Long Library after lunch. She browsed the shelves of more than five thousand leather-bound books dating back to the seventeenth century, and showed such an interest in the English classics that when she returned to Moscow Mum and Dad gave her a first edition of Thackeray's *Vanity Fair*. Dad showed her an octagonal table on which an inlaid brass plate reads: '*This Table belonged to Napoleon Bonaparte and was constantly used by him at St Helena to the day of his death 1822.*' The treasures housed in the walnut bureau always intrigued visitors. They included a Cromwell mask, a number of miniatures, and a ring which belonged to Elizabeth I. Chequers is fortunate to have a number of treasures related to Cromwell, thanks to the house passing to the Lord Protector's grandson John in 1715. There is a Cromwell Passage in the house – access is through a secret door in the bookshelves in the Long Gallery, a bit of theatre which greatly impressed me.

I used to sleep in the Prison Room, right up under the eaves. It was named because Lady Mary Grey, younger sister of Lady Jane Grey, was imprisoned here in 1565. Her 'crime' had been to marry a widower far below her station, a sergeant porter of the Royal Watergates at Westminster, without her family's consent. The last surviving grandchild of Mary Tudor, she was banished from court by Queen Elizabeth for two years. I felt tremendous sympathy for this diminutive girl, who had slept beneath the room's sloping ceilings more than four hundred years before me. Framed on the wall were some of her pitiful letters to the Queen begging to be released. Elizabeth, though, remained firm. She was determined to ensure that 'there were no little bastards' from what she and others considered to be an unlawful marriage. Her wish was granted: Lady Mary died childless at thirty-three.

My father particularly revelled in the more recent history of Chequers, including the fact that the Long Gallery had been used as a cinema by Winston Churchill during the Second World War. Apparently, Churchill watched the whole of *Gone with the Wind* with Foreign Secretary Anthony Eden one night, and then kept him up until dawn discussing the North Africa campaign. In the same room, Dad entertained Harold Macmillan early on in my mother's prime ministership. Sharing a bottle of champagne with Macmillan, while Mum was in her study running the country, he relished every minute of the former prime minister's company. Macmillan had apparently chided my mother for her inability to relax, advising her to read more, and warning her against overdoing things, a sentiment my father would have wholeheartedly endorsed.

Left alone with Dad, Macmillan took a trip down memory lane. 'His moustache rose and fell in time with the tempo of his tales,' Dad told me. 'He must have been over eighty but he had an enormous intellectual capacity, was extremely well-educated and quite fascinating. You would throw out a question or make a statement and before you could say "knife" he was back with Churchill and telling stories.'

Curled up on a comfy sofa at Chequers on a weekend

afternoon, while Dad was practising his chipping and putting out on the lawn and Mum was toiling away over her official red boxes, I often wished I could hop into Dr Who's time machine and whizz back to some of the most historic scenes in the history of the house. Which would I have chosen? Perhaps the 1942 visit of the Soviet delegation to discuss developments in the war; one of the delegates was Stalin's foreign minister, Vyacheslav Molotov, of Molotov cocktail fame.

The Russians were not the easiest house guests, according to reports. One housekeeper who knocked on Molotov's bedroom door and opened it was confronted by a loaded revolver pointing at her. Maids making the beds often came across more weapons under the pillows. Mealtimes were totally erratic, and the Russians often sat down hours late. One evening, when quail was on the menu, the small game birds had not been improved by the delay, and Winston Churchill announced: 'These miserable mice should never have been removed from Tutankhamen's tomb.'

We had some good times at Chequers even if my economical mother de-commissioned the indoor swimming pool, a gift from an American ambassador, when she discovered that the annual heating bill was £5,000. Renowned for her thrift, she would reply, 'On a shoe-string,' if anyone asked how Chequers was run. She herself didn't swim (ruinous to the hairdo), and she allocated the pool-heating money to the refurbishment of some attic bedrooms and the cupola in the Great Hall, and to cleaning the panelling in the Great Parlour.

Dad used to go for long walks, favouring those which ended up at licensed premises. Or he'd grab a couple of golf clubs, plant his brightly coloured umbrella upside down in the lawn, then – having paced out the requisite number of yards – start raining balls down on it. He did his best on Saturday nights to persuade Mum to abandon work in favour of a TV supper in the den-sized White Parlour.

Chequers had a marvellous caretaker, Wing Commander Vera Thomas, who saw to it that my parents had whatever they desired. She told the staff: 'If the prime minister or Mr Thatcher want moose on toast at midnight, they get it.' She knew my mother's weakness for chocolate, and indulged her. She also knew that my father lived largely on reheated meals or his favourite, beans on toast, during the week and so she spoiled him at weekends.

Chequers gave my parents the chance to live in a stately home; and an excuse to entertain friends and family, as well as the great and the good, without lifting a finger. Mum took particular care to include many of the staff and their families at Christmas and special celebrations, including Bob Goodwyn, Churchill's driver, who lived in one of the lodges, and various estate employees.

Having lunch in the glorious panelled dining room on a sunny day, overlooking the walled rose garden and the cows grazing in the Buckinghamshire countryside beyond, is magical. And Christmas at Chequers, when Mark and I would arrive on Christmas Eve and dump our presents under the floor-to-ceiling tree in the Great Hall, was very special. Cards from Royals and

VIPs were displayed on top of the grand piano. Guests would comment on official photos or signatures, often remarking on the problems some famous people had achieving joined-up writing. There would be a cocktail party in the Great Hall for about fifty people, including cabinet colleagues and MPs who lived nearby.

Then, having released her detectives to spend time with their families, on Christmas morning Mum and Dad went to Ellesborough church (where Dad had tactfully trained the vicar to shorten his sermons). We were usually about sixteen for Christmas lunch, which Mum always insisted we finished before the Queen's speech. It was a perfect roast dinner carved by the chef himself, Flight Sergeant Alan Lavender. The menu never varied: chilled melon, roast turkey with all the trimmings, followed by Christmas pudding, brandy sauce and mince pies.

At the end of our time in that wonderful house, I wandered round the garden for the last time with a heavy heart. I couldn't help but think of the words of Colonel Charles Russell, circa 1740: 'That dear delightful place, Chequers, where nothing but joy and tranquillity, health and pleasure can ever reign.' I reread the inscription on the sundial in the sunken rose garden:

Ye houres doe flie
Full soone we die,
In age secure
Ye House and Hills
Alone endure

In their forty years of marriage, Chequers was the house my parents lived in the longest, and their fondness for it never diminished. Ronnie Millar remembers happening upon my mother sitting on a stool before the fire in the Great Parlour. 'Sitting there like that,' he told her with a smile, 'you look for all the world as though you belong to Chequers and Chequers belongs to you.'

'But it doesn't,' my mother replied realistically.

I recall the time when Mark and I both managed to squeeze onto the end of the table for a splendid Sunday lunch held in honour of Princess Margaret. Chequers looked at its best, with roaring fires in the grates and elaborate flower arrangements on almost every surface. The meal was wonderful: delicious trout, roast saddle of lamb, fruit salad and cheese. Fellow guests included Norman Tebbit, Cecil Parkinson and Michael Heseltine, with their respective wives, along with Admiral Sir John Fieldhouse and Lady Fieldhouse, Antony Jay (writer of Mum's favourite television programme, Yes, Minister) and Professor Alan Walters, her economic adviser. It all went extremely well.

Once the Princess had left, we adjourned for coffee to the Long Library upstairs. Mum was soon on the warpath, talking of 'attack strategies' for the coming election (her second since taking office), and was in ebullient mood. When everyone had gone, though, she became somewhat wistful. Gazing out of the window at the idyllic pastoral scene, she said quietly, 'When I'm a private person – if we lose – I've had the best four years of one's life.' She paused and looked around the beautiful room. 'You do think, "Perhaps I won't be here again."'

Her sentiments echoed those of a previous incumbent, Lady Olwen Carey-Evans. On hearing of her father's defeat, she blurted out, 'Damn! There goes Chequers!'

I knew exactly how she felt.

Chapter Seven

CHOPPY WATERS

Y MAIN PRIORITY as the final week of March 1982 drew to a close was not to get caught out by an April Fool's Day prank. I'd just started a new job, as a journalist at the *Daily Telegraph* newspaper in London, and I wanted to make a good impression. There were plenty of people who disapproved of the prime minister and, as her daughter, I sometimes became a surrogate target.

I needn't have worried, though. It wasn't a mischievous colleague who wrong-footed me that week. It was General Leopoldo Galtieri of Argentina, who threw the lives of the Thatcher family (and those of a great many more in the seventy-four days that followed) into complete turmoil. Neither my parents nor I had ever been to Argentina. In fact, most of what I knew about the country came from Tim Rice and Andrew Lloyd Webber's musical *Evita*, about the life of its legendary First Lady, Eva Perón.

On Wednesday, 31 March, my mother was working in her office at the House of Commons when she received a request for an emergency cabinet meeting from John Nott, secretary of state for defence. He told her and the rest of the hastily convened cabinet that the Argentine fleet was sailing towards the Falkland Islands and that an invasion was imminent.

Two days later, on Friday, 2 April – grateful at having survived April Fool's Day intact – I was enjoying a drink with friends in a pub near my Fulham home, completely unaware of what was about to unfold. My father was in the drawing room of the private flat on the top floor of Number Ten, Downing Street, nursing a gin and tonic. He was interrupted by a message from the prime minister's office: the Falklands had been invaded. 'I remember checking in *The Times Atlas of the World*, to find out where the bloody hell they were,' he said later, 'and I wasn't the only one.'

In the chaotic days that followed, rumours were rife that some of the powers-that-be in Whitehall had instructed their staff to consult train and ferry timetables to the Falkland Islands – under the impression that they were located a few miles from Orkney, off the northern coast of Scotland. There was nothing light-hearted, however, about the media coverage my mother's government received the following morning. The *Daily Mail*'s front page was headlined 'Shamed!' and spoke of a 'Falklands fiasco'. Photographs showed the Union Flag being lowered outside Government House in Port Stanley, and Marines surrendering to Argentine forces. Peter Carrington, the foreign secretary, was held largely to blame, but my mother was also in the firing line.

She had been prime minister for almost four years, but I had never seen her in action, so to speak, in the House of Commons. Whenever I'd asked if I could sit in the public gallery during the weekly Prime Minister's Questions, she'd replied that she'd rather not have members of the family there. She didn't want the distraction of looking up, mid-flow, and spotting one of us. That morning, the television news reported that the Commons would sit in emergency session – the first Saturday sitting since Suez in 1956. Listening to such talk, I really thought the government might fall and my ma would be out of a job.

This was something I simply couldn't wait out at home. If things were as bad as they seemed, this might be my last opportunity to see my mother on the front line of politics. Deciding not to ask through prime ministerial channels for a ticket to the public gallery, I took matters into my own hands and jumped on the Tube to Westminster. As I walked down Whitehall towards the Commons, I threw a glance towards Number Ten, picking up on the black mood I could feel enveloping the place.

Joining the queue of like-minded people, all eager to witness this moment in history, I was fortunate enough to get in. Happily, no one seemed to recognise me. The Chamber was packed. MPs were standing in the aisles. The feeling of occasion was tangible. The buck, as the Americans would say, stopped with my mother. As she rose to the despatch box, I don't think I have ever felt sorrier for her. She said later that the mood in the House that day was 'the most difficult I ever had to face'.

I should have known better than to worry. Emphatically, she told parliament, 'The House meets this Saturday to respond to a situation of great gravity. We are here because, for the first time for many years, British sovereign territory has been invaded by a foreign power ... I am sure that this House will join me in condemning totally this unprovoked aggression by the government of Argentina against British territory.'

'Hear! Hear!' people cried, and I began to relax a little.

Her voice took on a harder edge. 'The Falkland Islands and their dependencies remain British territory. No aggression and no invasion can alter that simple fact. It is the government's objective to see that the islands are freed from occupation and returned to British administration at the earliest possible moment.'

As the papers had already been full of the logistical difficulties of retaking islands so far away, I couldn't help but wonder how on earth we were going to achieve that, but Mum didn't lack resolve and her response seemed to be going down well. There were, of course, dissenters. One Labour MP, questioning the wisdom of sending British troops to war, described part of the islands as 'a piece of rock in the most southerly of the dependencies which is completely uninhabited and which smells of large accumulations of penguins' and other bird droppings'.

Defending her decision not to do anything about the crisis sooner, Mum replied: 'There is only a British Antarctic scientific survey there and there was a commercial contract (given to an Argentinian company) to remove a whaling station. I suggest . . . that had I come to the House at that time and said that we had a problem on South Georgia with ten people who had landed with a contract to remove a whaling station, and had I gone on to say that we should send HMS *Invincible*, I should have been accused of war-mongering and sabre-rattling.'

Enoch Powell got to his feet and, as Mum recalled it, 'looked directly across the Chamber and declared sepulchrally: "The Prime Minister, shortly after she came into office, received a soubriquet as the 'Iron Lady' . . . In the next week or two, this House, the nation, and the Right Honourable Lady herself will learn of what metal she is made."'

(Some time later, when the war was won, Enoch Powell revisited his metallic theme in parliament. 'Is the Right Honourable Lady aware that the report has now been received from the public analyst on a certain substance recently subjected to analysis and that I have obtained a copy of the report?' he said, his tongue clearly in his cheek. 'It shows that the substance under test consisted of ferrous matter of the highest quality, and that it is of exceptional tensile strength, is highly resistant to wear and tear and to stress, and may be used to advantage for all national purposes.'

She was so chuffed by Powell's quote that her devoted parliamentary private secretary, Ian Gow, had it framed for her as a Christmas present, which hung on her office wall thereafter.)

After the emergency Commons debate that Saturday, I made my way to Number Ten in sombre mood. As I walked past the Cenotaph, with all its connotations of previous wars Britain has fought, I half imagined packing up my parents' belongings. Early in my childhood, I'd got the message very clearly about tied cottages: they go with the job, and that means the occupants may have to move out pretty rapidly. Over the years Mum and I had devised a simple system which would help speed things up should a lightning departure ever be needed. I had stuck little stars (like the ones children get in school) on anything which belonged to our family as opposed to HM Government. To ensure they weren't too obvious, I placed them out of sight, on the bottom of lamps or clocks, for example.

In the front hall of Number Ten, the house manager greeted me with a nod towards some building work in progress around the entrance to the lift. 'Preparations for sandbagging,' he quipped. I half expected to see blackout curtains being installed.

I found my mother in the sitting room. There was no sign of doubt on her face. This was Britain's first female prime minister auditioning for the part of war leader.

'Are you OK?' I asked gingerly.

'Fine,' she replied, stuffing her hands into the pockets of her dress. 'We're down now but not for long. I've just been downstairs and told Peter [Carrington] and John [Nott] that we're going to fight back.' She continued where she'd left off in the Commons, although this time I was her only audience. I had never seen every fibre of a person so committed to the fight. She was resolution in power heels.

Later that afternoon she and Dad drove to Chequers, but they didn't stay long. She returned from church on Sunday morning, marched purposefully across the Great Hall and announced, 'I'm going back to London. I know we can win.' Referring to talk of a possible compromise with the Argentinians, she added, 'If they won't go, we'll throw them off.' Right up to the surrender of Stanley almost three months later, she had complete tunnel vision.

On 5 April 1982, amid fervent flag-waving and much patriotic music, the Royal Navy task force set sail from Portsmouth on the two-week voyage to the South Atlantic. The fleet was led by the carriers HMS *Invincible* and HMS *Hermes*, and included eleven destroyers and frigates and an amphibious assault ship, HMS *Fearless*. With support vessels and troop-carriers, some of which sailed later, over a hundred ships carrying twenty-five thousand men were despatched to war. It was Britain's greatest display of naval strength since the Suez crisis.

My mother barely rested in what she later described as 'the most totally concentrated period of my life'. She braced herself for every telephone call or missive, in case it was bad news. At Chequers, she'd look across green fields full of cattle grazing in the spring sunshine and say, almost to herself, 'It's such a lovely day here. You just wonder what they're going through down there.' She didn't despair, though, even when the news was bad. 'I never doubted that what we were doing was right,' she said. In that, she had the wholehearted support of my father, an ex-soldier, whose attitude matched hers.

'From the word go, I said, "Send them off!"' he recalled later. 'I never had any doubts that we were going to win, but it was such an enormous operation . . .'

Britain seemed to rally round her, and so did I – emotionally, at least. She was so busy with the business of war; there was little time for family. Long able, like her hero Winston Churchill, to survive on a few hours sleep, now she was snatching only the odd hour here and there, often sitting up all night to listen to the BBC World Service or waiting for bulletins delayed by the time difference. I remember her operating virtually on autopilot.

I would walk into the flat and say, 'Hello, Mum. How are you?'

'Hello, darling,' she'd reply, without raising her head. When I walked out again, I doubt if she even realised I'd been there.

The war cabinet met daily. It included Francis Pym, who succeeded Peter Carrington as foreign secretary after the latter's resignation, Home Secretary Willie Whitelaw, Tory party chairman Cecil Parkinson and John Nott, as well as Admiral Sir John Fieldhouse, commander-in-chief of the fleet, and Sir Terence Lewin, chief of defence staff. One of their hottest topics was the problem of getting supplies to the armed forces once they were in situ. Wanting to do my bit, I offered to cook dinner for a few of them at Number Ten one night, but as I drove my battered Ford Fiesta along Birdcage Walk, the engine spluttered and died. Leaping out with two carrier bags full of food, I jumped into a cab.

'Ten Downing Street,' I yelled, painfully aware of the clock ticking. Normally, I was much vaguer about my destination, asking the driver to drop me in 'Whitehall, somewhere near the corner of Downing Street,' and only sloping inside once they'd driven off, but this was an emergency. The war chiefs were gathered in the small dining room of my parents' private flat when I burst in, breathlessly. 'My car broke down,' I apologised. 'The supply problems begin here.'

I think the toughest part for Mum was the lack of information, especially when she was so desperate for news. Having given the order to go to war, she had resolved to leave the generals and admirals alone and not ring them up constantly to ask how the campaign was going. I remember her saying, 'I wish I knew, I wish I knew,' and my father calmly replying, 'This is how it is in a war.' His role as morale-booster and nerve-calmer was invaluable. He described the mood at Number Ten during that difficult time very well: 'We were living in a goldfish bowl, facing a new crisis every day.'

Thanks in part to him, my mother's coolness during the conflict was astonishing. On 2 May, news came in that the Argentine cruiser *General Belgrano* had been torpedoed and sunk, with the loss of three hundred and twenty-one lives. My mother staunchly defended her decision to sanction the firing of the torpedoes, claiming that otherwise she would have endangered the lives of British personnel. Even when it was later discovered that the *Belgrano* had been sailing away from the Task Force when she was sunk, my mother insisted that the threat was real and the order to sink her correct, a view she maintains to this day.

On the third anniversary of Mum's becoming prime minister, I arrived at Number Ten with a bottle of champagne. I felt this was something that should be celebrated, despite the crisis and the accompanying upheaval. Mum tends to drink the occasional Scotch, but will sometimes sip champagne to join in a toast. I put the bottle in the fridge in the laundry room and went looking for her. Her staff informed me that she wouldn't be home until very late. The British destroyer HMS *Sheffield* had been hit by an Argentine Exocet missile. More than twenty men were missing, feared dead. I left the champagne in the fridge – where it remained for several months – and returned home with a heavy heart.

On 21 May, the day five thousand British troops landed in San Carlos Bay in the Falklands, my mother attended a constituency function, smiling, waving and clutching a bouquet of flowers. I saw her photograph in the papers the following day. Visiting Number Ten later that night, I said: 'Crikey, why on earth did you go to Finchley yesterday? And how could you smile like that? I mean, how could you have looked so calm?'

She admitted it had been an exercise in self-control. 'Of course, all my thoughts were in the South Atlantic,' she told me. 'I was desperately worried; it was just so important that the landing went right. But if I hadn't gone to the function, people would have thought something was wrong. I had to carry on as normal.'

Thankfully, the landing was successful, and most of the troops reached the shore safely, despite a heavy air bombardment. There was more bad news to come, not least the losses of HMS *Coventry*, the *Atlantic Conveyor* supply ship, two landing-ships, *Sir Tristram* and *Sir Galahad*, and the attack on HMS *Glamorgan*, but our soldiers fought their way steadily onwards.

Late on the night of Monday, 14 June, I was driving home when I heard my mother's voice on the car radio and turned up the volume. 'They [Argentine soldiers] are reported to be flying white flags over Port Stanley,' she told the House of Commons. Slamming on the brakes and pulling over, I cheered, along with delighted MPs and just about everyone else who heard the news that day. My main emotion was relief for my mother. I had seen little of her in the previous days, but images of her leaving Number Ten dressed in black, on her way to give bad news to the House, showed me the strain she was under.

Returning to Downing Street later that night, my parents bade goodnight to the policeman guarding the door and went inside. My father recalled, 'As we walked past the famous bulldog portrait of Winston [Churchill] . . . I swear the great man bowed and said, "Well done, girl."'

With two hundred and fifty-five British dead, and almost six hundred and fifty Argentine servicemen and three Falklanders killed, the war had taken its toll on everyone involved. As for my mother, my father said simply: 'The Falklands marked her soul – and mine.'

In late 2006, almost a quarter of a century later, I decided to make my own pilgrimage to the Falkland Islands to talk to as many people as I could who had been there at the time. I had hundreds of questions which had been building up over the years, and the approaching twenty-fifth anniversary seemed the ideal time to go in search of the answers. I wanted to know what it felt like to be under Argentine occupation, what the islanders had done to help the British soldiers, and what their lives were like now. These people have always had a special place in my mother's heart and I wanted to meet some of them face to face.

There are two ways of flying to the Falklands. One is the weekly flight from Santiago in Chile, which makes various stops, sometimes including one in Argentinian Patagonia, before the final three-hundred-mile hop north-east of Cape Horn. The other, and the path I took, is a flight from RAF Brize Norton in Oxfordshire, with a stop at Ascension Island before a ten-hour flight in the direction of the South Pole. This is colloquially known as the 'air bridge'. Flying high above the ocean, I settled down in my seat to read my *Lonely Planet* guide to the islands. A fellow passenger was surprised. As the daughter of Margaret Thatcher, didn't I already know everything there was to know about this windswept outcrop in the South Atlantic? Didn't I have such details etched on my heart and soul? Fair comment, I acknowledged. Yes, I knew the islands' chequered history, and felt a close connection to the islanders, having thought about little else during those traumatic weeks of war, but I had never visited before and lacked local knowledge.

During the short transit stop in Ascension, I spotted an open-air picnic area alongside the tarmac, a spot locally dubbed 'the Cage'. A couple of teenagers waiting there recognised me from my recent stint on *I'm a Celebrity*, and introduced themselves. One played the trombone and the other the saxophone in their school orchestra back in England. They were off on a concert tour of the Falklands. My first reaction was sheer astonishment at the exotic nature of modern school trips, in comparison to the rather tame excursions of my generation. The furthest I ever went from boarding school was to visit Big Ben.

As these teenagers had been born a decade after the conflict, I asked what they knew of the islands. The trombone player revealed that her father had seen service there in the armed forces. His take on the weather, she informed me, was that it was less windy and cold in their summer than in their winter. Luckily, we were heading into the warmer season.

Several hours later, we began our descent into Port Stanley. My first impression from the air was surprise at how parched and brown the islands looked in comparison to the rain and snow-soaked bogs over which our troops had been filmed yomping so admirably twenty-five years earlier. Disembarking, however, it became clear the friendly advice on the weather was rather wide of the mark: the wind was so strong that it almost knocked me off my feet.

I headed straight for Stanley, my base for the next ten days, and checked into my hotel. The town was exactly as my parents, who'd visited in 1983 and 1992, had described it to me: a small settlement of clapboard houses, with red telephone boxes, six pubs and an unmistakable British character. The following morning, I went to the old airport on the fringes of Stanley, from where the small inter-island flights still depart. In the control tower I talked to pensioner Gerald Cheek, who had been the head of civil aviation back in 1982. From his control tower, he directed my binoculars to the spot where the Argentinians had first landed at eleven o'clock at night on 1 April, and described how they had advanced towards the capital. Looking at the scene, all the turbulent emotions I'd felt at the shocking news of the invasion resurfaced. It had taken my mother and the government completely by surprise.

The day after the invasion, Gerald Cheek was one of a number of people rounded up from their homes by Argentine soldiers and driven to the airport, unsure of what their fate would be. To his horror, there was a Hercules sitting on the tarmac with its engines running. Shivers ran down his spine. Was he about to be shipped off to Argentina? Would they ever arrive? Or were they about to join the ranks of the thirty thousand or so 'desaparecidos', the men, women and children who vanished during the reign of the military junta between 1976 and 1983 in what is still known as that country's 'Dirty War'? Mercifully, those rounded up were ferried instead to Fox Bay, a farm on West Falkland, where they remained for the duration of the war.

A fellow hostage was Brian Summers, a communications technician, who had been in charge of the telex in Government House. Argentine troops marched him out of his office within hours of their landing. 'There was a knock on the door and when I opened it, an Argentine soldier was standing there,' recalled Brian. 'He gestured – he didn't speak English – to the road outside.' Along with some of the Royal Marines stationed at Government House who had surrendered, Brian was forced to lie down in the road a few feet from the waterfront. He showed me the place where enemy vehicles had rumbled past the defeated and humiliated British. Their dilemma was whether to get up and risk being shot by the Argentine guards, or remain on the ground and hope the traffic didn't run them over.

The Argentinians had made the Brits empty their pockets of wallets, keys and other personal belongings and then – rather petulantly – chucked them into the thick hedges of gorse, leaving their owners to dig around and retrieve them later. During the tense and nervy hours of the initial takeover, the Argentinians also announced a no-smoking policy. As an act of defiance, even non-smoking prisoners, who normally wouldn't have touched the weed if you'd paid them, lit up any cigarettes they could lay their hands on.

Looking back, Brian said, his trip to the airport to be deported to Fox Bay had been pure farce, although fear of the unknown prevented him from seeing the funny side at the time. He and his two Argentine minders set off in his Mini - of which he was inordinately proud because it was the only one on the island - but disagreed over which side of the road they ought to be driving on. The locals drove on the left, the occupiers on the right. In the end, they compromised and drove in the middle. As they rounded a corner, the Mini almost collided with an Argentine army truck crammed with soldiers. Brian said his minders turned very pale at the prospect of swerving off into one of the newly laid minefields.

Other islanders told me tales of incredible ingenuity. At the small settlement of whitewashed houses at Goose Green, the site of the first major land battle of the war, I sat riveted as Willy Bowles described how he and a hundred other residents, including children, were held prisoner in the community hall for three weeks. Reading from his diary, Willy - who spoke Spanish and liaised with their captors - said that the Argentinians had confiscated all radios although two locals somehow managed to hang on to one. Showing considerable courage and initiative, these radio buffs took the radio apart to make it easier to hide. Then every night they put it back together and surreptitiously tuned in to the BBC to get news of how the war was progressing.

I studied my parents' signatures in the islands' visitors' book and recalled the cloak-and dagger operation that had surrounded their first visit there, six months after the war. Mum and Dad left Number Ten that day with their bags as if they were going to

Chequers as normal for the weekend. Instead, they were whisked off to Brize Norton, where a VC-10 was waiting to take them to Ascension Island. When they finally arrived in the Falklands, their welcome was astonishingly warm. Almost the entire population came out to greet them, and Union Flags were waved enthusiastically. Governor Sir Rex Hunt took them into Port Stanley in his famous London taxi, and they then visited all the major battle grounds, visibly moved by what they saw.

Everybody I met twenty-five years later was still full of grateful praise for my mother. I was disappointed to learn that I was a few weeks too early to celebrate the public holiday Margaret Thatcher Day on 10 January. Almost everyone had a tale to tell. I spoke to one man whose wife and child had been relocated out of Stanley for safety. They were sent to a farm right on the shores of San Carlos Bay. British spotters scanning the scene through binoculars from ships lying off shore told them later that the sight of island children playing on the beach confirmed that there were no mines lying in wait.

Visiting the Falklands after all this time, I felt like someone with a slowly developing Polaroid; at last, everything I'd read and heard came into focus. The day I went to San Carlos Bay, the weather was of South Atlantic perfection: the cobalt-blue sky met the flat blue of the sea. The sun blazed and it was hot. Gary Clements, a Marine now married to a Falklander, took me to the place where he'd first come ashore. The Marines' eighty-mile march carrying full kit was a miracle of modern warfare. Having seen for myself the hostile terrain they had to cross after landing at San Carlos Bay, I had even more respect for their heroic effort. I don't believe any other force in the world would have had the physical or mental strength to carry it off.

It said much about the fast and frantic nature of the landing that Gary – a bald, broad-shouldered individual with a goatee beard – couldn't remember whether he had come in by landing craft or helicopter. 'Not long after we got ashore, we had our first air-raid warning,' he told me. 'People were blowing whistles left, right and centre and everybody took cover. All of a sudden everything was very, very real and we knew we were into something that was far worse than we expected.' He walked me through a collection of derelict, corrugated-iron sheds and outbuildings which had once provided some of the only cover the troops had throughout the war. They had originally been built as an abattoir and processing plant when sheep prices had been good. The plant had only functioned for a few years.

The atmosphere was spooky. One shed had been used by the troops to detain Argentine PoWs. I hauled open one of the thick, heavy doors which had once been the entrance to the refrigerated warehouse. During the war, it doubled as a basic (not to say Spartan) military hospital. The gallant and dedicated medics had carried on treating the injured even when a hundred-pound bomb lodged itself in the roof right above the operating theatre. Mercifully it didn't explode. Others were not so lucky during the same raid. 'I watched four bombs drop off the bottom of an

Argentine fighter jet and dived in a hole, thinking, "There's nothing more I can do," ' Gary said. 'There was a lot of smoke and fire and a lot of screaming going on. Four people were killed, including one crewman on the frigate HMS *Antelope*.

A few yards from the hospital entrance, a rookery of noisy Gentoo penguins scuttled around. During the war their little patch of ground had been the helipad. When choppers put down with their lights blazing, that was the signal that there were casualties on board. All spare raced to be stretcher bearers. I squinted in the sunshine across the sparkling water to where a buoy marks the spot where HMS *Antelope* sank after being hit in a bombing raid.

I met people who had been marched around at Argentine gunpoint, others whose first tangible contact with the war had been answering a knock on the door and hearing the reassuring words, 'Don't worry, I'm Kevin from Great Britain.' There were individual acts of courage on the part of the Falkland islanders as well. Many used tractors, trailers and Land Rovers to move troops and ammunition because helicopters were lost when the supply ship *Atlantic Conveyor* was sunk. Near the wreckage of an Argentine helicopter, I met Trudi McPhee, a doughty and spirited sheep farmer who was nicknamed 'Taskforce Trudi' for the invaluable help she gave the British troops. From the word go, patriotic Trudi's attitude had been that Argentinians occupying her veggie garden simply wasn't on.

After a lunch of the best slow-cooked leg of mutton I'll ever taste, she recounted how she had agreed to guide a long convoy of military vehicles, across terrain where only local knowledge could avoid the bogs and other hazards, to the frontline mountains overlooking Stanley. Making extremely slow progress at nothing quicker than walking speed, Trudi used a pair of white woollen gloves held behind her back to allow the driver of the lead truck to follow her in total darkness on a journey that took all night. She also carried a stick of morphine. 'They told me to plunge it into my leg and that would kill the pain if I ever got hit,' she told me. 'Then I was to wait until they could get me some more help.' She still had the gloves and the stick of morphine, as mementoes.

Soon after Trudi's heroics, Port Stanley fell and the war was over. Now things are very different in the Falklands, which have undergone an economic transformation since the conflict. People fly off for golfing weekends in Santiago; *Penguin News*, the local paper in Stanley, carries ads for pop concerts; and the sale of fishing licences has poured millions of pounds into the islands' economy. Even the sheep farmers, who used to live in isolation with part-time generators, now have constant power. Many of them hire out their sturdy 4x4s to take visiting cruise-ship passengers to see penguins or eat cream teas. For Trudi McPhee, though, not that much had changed. She told her story as if it had happened yesterday. After our delicious lunch, she led me out into the warm December sunshine when the summer days were so long that the locals joked that it was only worth putting their Christmas tree lights on in the couple of hours of darkness at midnight. I helped her collect eggs from her hens and enquired where they would be going. 'To the British Antarctic Survey station,' Trudi replied matter-of-factly.

I couldn't believe it. It wasn't just any old customer that was going to be eating these top-quality speckled eggs that I was juggling so carefully. More than a generation on from when the captain of a British Antarctic Survey ship first picked up a ham radio broadcast and passed the news to the Foreign Office that the invasion of the Falkland Islands was under way, I was holding in my hand eggs bound for the same station. Sometimes it's the simplest things in life that complete the circle.

I had gone on this journey to find out what had happened in the war and, for me that meant talking to people from both sides, no matter how hostile their reaction might be. So, on my way home, I flew to Buenos Aires to meet Argentine war veterans and the mothers of men who lost their lives on the *General Belgrano*. I was greeted by a noisy demonstration at the airport, with protesters carrying banners ordering me to 'Go Home' and branding my mother a war criminal. I met the veterans in a tango hall and discovered that their views had not softened over time.

'What is ours must be returned to us,' they told me, defiantly. 'During our lifetime we hope to see our flag flying again over our territory.'

'Don't you respect the islanders' wishes to be British?' I asked.

'No,' came the resounding reply.

One woman whose son died on the *Belgrano* said, 'I never saw him again because your mother killed him.' Another asked, 'Do you know how it feels when Christmas and birthdays come and your hands are empty? I didn't even have my son's body to cry over.'

I decided to be firm and I refused to apologise on behalf of my mother. There was a war on, which the Argentines had started, the *Belgrano* was a possible threat to British ships, and my mother had no alternative but to authorise its sinking. Not surprisingly, they didn't agree. 'Some day God will punish you,' one told me. I hoped that in venting their feelings on me, these veterans and mothers felt they had in some way fought back against those they held responsible and found some sort of closure.

Chapter Eight

MAKING WAVES

THE EARLY 1980s were among the toughest periods of my mother's premiership. Even before the Falklands war, there had been problems at home.

Having embarked on a radical series of reforms which included slashing public spending and confronting trade union abuses, she was hampered by a world-wide recession. Even after reshuffling her cabinet, Mum faced obstacles, including some disastrous by-election results and violent summer riots in Brixton, Bristol, Moss Side and Toxteth. The damaging year-long miners' strike loomed, in protest at planned pit closures and the castration of the all-powerful unions.

When I returned to Britain at the end of 1981, Mum and Dad

had been at Number Ten for three years. I'd taken over our old home in Flood Street, which my parents no longer used, until I bought my own place in Fulham. Few people noticed my return, thankfully. I was not nearly as newsworthy as Mark whose motor-racing and business exploits had already earned him a number of mentions in the tabloids. Mark's choice of recreation didn't win the unstinting approval of either parent, but both had their hands full and, having rarely interfered in our upbringing, were hardly going to start laying down the law now.

In January 1982, two years after successfully completing the gruelling Le Mans twenty-four-hour race, Mark signed up for the even more gruelling Paris–Dakar rally. He was to drive a Peugeot 504 with co-driver Charlotte Verney and mechanic Jean Garnier. Crossing the Sahara Desert, on 9 January the trio became separated from a convoy of two other cars when they stopped to repair a rear axle near the border between Algeria and Mali. The following day, a Sunday, we received a message from the *Daily Express*. They told us there were reports that Mark had gone missing. It was long before the days of satellite telephones and locator beacons. We learned later that Mark and his crew had just five litres of water and a little dried food to sustain them in the searing desert heat. No one panicked at first, because we felt sure we would have heard if it was anything serious, and anyway the French rally organisers told us that they had set up a search operation, and were in the process of rescuing the team.

Communications were slow and garbled, but by Tuesday

evening, Derek Howe, a member of Mum's political staff, came up to the flat and explained to Dad and me that Mark was still missing and that it was another competitor who had been rescued. The colour drained from Dad's face. 'Christ!' he said. 'Margaret will go spare. We'd better go down to the study.'

The newspapers had a field day. The headlines screamed: *'Prime Minister's Son Missing'*. Mum was said to be 'very upset and distressed', and 'under obvious strain'. Reporters and television crews were flown to the scene. It was the first time Mark managed to knock Mum off the front pages.

Dad was right. Mum fell apart. Throughout the ordeal, she was completely unable to function. One night, I found her surrounded by red boxes and close to tears as she read a note from the editor of one daily newspaper: 'How we hope we will be able to lead our paper tomorrow with the news that your son has been found.'

A few days later, Dad was sitting in the bath early one morning, contemplating the busy day ahead, when Mum hammered on the door. She had news. Hector Laing (later Lord Laing, chairman of United Biscuits) had offered his plane. 'You can fly down to Tamanrasset to look for Mark,' she said, through the door. Tamanrasset is deep in the Algerian Sahara.

All plans were cancelled and, within hours, and despite his own deep reluctance, my sixty-six-year-old father found himself flying off into the sandy yonder. He telephoned from some far-flung outpost to reassure us that an extensive ground and air search was under way, using Hercules aircraft loaned from the Algerian air force. Mum had already been on the phone to the British ambassador in Algiers. Twenty-four hours later, six days after they had first gone missing, Mark and his team were found, unharmed.

Unshaven, and bemused by all the fuss, Mark greeted Dad rather too casually. 'Hello,' he said. 'What are you doing here?'

Dad, his face like thunder, held his tongue until Mark mentioned that he would like to go on and finish the rally. 'Not bloody likely!' Dad snapped.

When word came through that Mark was safe, Mum went up to the flat to watch the lunchtime news, which showed him scruffily announcing that there had been a great deal of fuss about nothing. Mum announced that she would like a drink. The telephone rang and Crawfie answered. It was her friend Ronald Reagan, offering his congratulations.

The entire episode stamped Mark with a 'lost in the Sahara' image and for a while every stand-up comic recycled the incident. When Mum went to Moscow shortly afterwards, even Mr Gorbachev joined in. 'Why didn't you bring your son along?' he asked, adding mischievously, 'We've got plenty of deserts for him to get lost in.'

There was, at least, one benefit. The rest of us could relax a little because Mark had hung an 'Occupied' sign on the family's Embarrassing Relative slot. (I deservedly got that slot too when I omitted to pay the poll tax, which, unsurprisingly, also made headlines.)

*

By the end of 1982, having led the country to victory during the Falklands war a few months after Mark's jaunt in the desert, my mother was riding high again in the polls. So when the next general election was set for 9 June the following year, I had the idea to write a book, to be published within a week of Polling Day, and entitled *Diary of an Election*. My objective was to tell the story from inside the goldfish bowl, as well as answer the question so often asked of me: 'What is it like to be the prime minister's daughter?'

Obviously, I had to ask Mum whether I would be able to follow the campaign team around. I knew, too, that I was in a no-win situation: I'd be damned if I did, and damned if I didn't. I was going to face accusations that I was using my position as the prime minister's daughter for professional and personal gain. If I gave in to those critics and dropped the idea of the book, my friends would rightly tell me that I was passing up a unique opportunity. With Mum's blessing, I decided to go for it. In addition to writing the book, I promised to make myself useful as my mother's underdogsbody and fourth-reserve wardrobe mistress.

Before we left, I helped sort out the clothes she would need on the gruelling three-week campaign. My mother had long been in favour of such meticulous advance organisation because it saved time later. My briefing began with a conducted tour of the relevant clothes, which were arranged in spare-room wardrobes. Cupboard One featured a selection of navy and black suits. 'I am expected to look executive,' she explained. I had to memorise which blouse went with which suit and which shoes fitted which occasion. Her choice of shoes was either 'clodhoppers' for walkabouts or comfortable ones for standing and making speeches. I stared at the racks of almost identical shoes growing on dozens of shoe-trees at the bottom of the cupboard and wondered how I was supposed to tell the difference. Fortunately, the 'speech shoes' – mostly suede court shoes – were in neatly labelled boxes in Cupboard Two.

Cupboard Three contained her best Aquascutum suits, never to be used on walkabouts because of the risk that she might be pelted with eggs, tomatoes or other missiles. These were for television interviews and had been chosen because they looked best on the screen (checks and stripes flicker). Each outfit had a nickname. These included 'Aubergine' for her purple suit, 'Cloudy' for the one featuring white squirls on black, and 'English Garden' for a pattern which resembled a herbaceous border. Cupboard Four contained dresses for evenings and rallies. When I spotted a navy polka-dot dress, I pointed out that we already had one like that. 'No,' she chided, sternly. 'This is navy chiffon spot, see-through. That was navy *silk* spot.' I was beginning to get a headache.

Then there were the outfits that had to be packed for a specific event – like the beige creation fashioned from a bolt of cloth a woollens factory had presented her with some time previously, and which she was determined to wear on her return visit. And there had to be nothing red (Labour's colour) and nothing with a foreign name or the words 'Made in ... Somewhere Overseas' visible anywhere on it. When your election address includes the maxim 'British is Best', and the press are likely to inspect the tyres on campaign buses to make sure they're home-produced, you can't be a walking advert for foreign competitors.

Even for a relatively straightforward overnight stay, I had to make sure that her suitcase was packed with reserve day clothes (in case of accident), a change for the evening, spare tights, spare shoes, evening shoes, Wellington boots, a (matching) scarf to protect the hairdo from the rain, near-industrial quantities of hairspray, and her indispensable heated rollers. In addition, I mustn't forget her white beauty case and her all-important briefcase.

I began to develop a secret dread about her clothes, terrified that I would never be able to coordinate her schedule with her outfits. I could foresee Mum arriving at a metalwork factory in the Midlands with only a sparkly evening dress to wear. While I was pulling my hair out, writing lists and trying to get everything prepared, my father was practising his golf swing, composure itself. Swing-o-meters, floating voters, slogans, spin doctors and manifestos were of little interest. When the time came, he'd be there by my mother's side when he needed to be, or 'working the other side of the street' during a walkabout, the perfect consort. Nobody ever offered to help him decide what clothes he wanted to pack.

One of our biggest concerns was the impending rehearsals for Trooping the Colour and Beating the Retreat on Horse Guards Parade. They rehearsed at the crack of dawn, right outside Mum and Dad's bedroom window, robbing them of the few hours' sleep they were able to snatch during pit stops home between campaign engagements. The schedule didn't look good – in fact, it clashed horribly, but there was nothing that could be done. She must have felt that pageantry and politics had conspired to deprive her of her sleep.

Before I left Number Ten on the eve of the campaign, I walked down the main staircase, whose walls are lined with the portraits of all the previous prime ministers. Looking at them, I realised that none of the sixteen PMs of the twentieth century, from Balfour to Callaghan, had won a consecutive second term. If my mother was to be the first, she would have set yet another remarkable historical precedent.

In the run-up to any general election there are always scandals, scams and smears, not to mention people losing their nerve. For me, though, 1983 had a carnival feel, because the polls looked good right from the beginning, giving the Tories a healthy 21 per cent lead. A new Conservative Party logo – described as 'an Olympic flame with a blue rinse' – had been devised and headed all notepaper and literature, to largely good reviews. The slogan 'Best Hope for Britain' had been adopted; there was a huge campaign bus which would serve as office-cum-campaign headquarters on the road; and Mum's horrible cold had passed, thank goodness, although she was still fortifying her voice with hot lemon and honey.

We even had a jaunty theme tune for the campaign, which Ronnie Millar had created by re-working the famous lyrics to the song 'Hello, Dolly'. It went like this:

Hello, Maggie,

Well, hello, Maggie,

Now you're really on the road to Number Ten.

You're growing strong, Maggie,

'Til you turn the key,

Then, Mrs T,

You'll see Big Ben,

All wreathed in smiles, Maggie,

In the aisles, Maggie,

There'll be dancing on that very special day,

So, here's to you, Maggie,

Give 'em the old one-two, Maggie,

Maggie, we're right behind you all the way!

Despite the optimistic reports flowing in and the terrific reception she received all around the country, my mother believed elections can always be lost unless you go flat out to the finishing line – which, of course, she did.

On the morning the campaign officially started, Thursday 19 May, I was to follow her up to Finchley (her first port of call), in my car, taking Joy Robilliard with me. We were the fourth car in the official convoy and sat with the engine revving outside Number Ten, ready for the off. In a flash, Mum swept out of the front door and straight into the back seat of her official car, which was waiting with its engine running. The door slammed and it moved swiftly off. The back-up car, containing prime ministerial staff followed, then Mark, who was hitching a ride with Mum's security men. I fell in behind them in a start which was more than a little like Formula One cars leaving the grid.

Driving in a fast-moving prime ministerial convoy was a nerve-racking experience, not least for my passenger, Joy, though she remained remarkably calm. I tried to stay dangerously close to car Number Three as it ducked in and out of the rush-hour traffic in Park Lane. Being an undercover police car, its occupants had a handy little sign saying 'POLICE' which they could wave at sluggish drivers they needed to move aside. I had no such sign, obviously, but made a mental note that if I was going to have to do much of this agile motor-racing around town, I'd get one printed saying 'ME TOO'.

We eventually arrived at Finchley to face a wall of lights, cameras and reporters, all creating a hothouse atmosphere, with cameramen walking backwards and tripping over themselves to get their shot of Mum. If this was a taste of things to come, I was really going to have to keep my wits about me.

The routine usually went something like this:

8 a.m. Conservative Central Office in Smith Square for a briefing.

9 a.m. Daily news conference and media interviews with anyone from Sue Lawley or Jean Rook to Walter Cronkite.

10 a.m. Departure by bus, train, plane or helicopter to that day's campaign destination, which could be anything from a

dumper-truck factory to an old people's home, via a hospital, school or supermarket.

6 p.m. After a full day of 'pressing the flesh', drumming up support among potential voters and showing her support for British industry, Mum would then have to attend a dinner or a rally or a television studio, involving yet another speech, yet another outfit, yet another bank of photographers.

Then it would be back to Number Ten late at night to kick off her shoes and curl up on the sofa until the small hours, going through her red boxes and the business of actually running the country.

Everything was timed to the second (we were allotted six seconds to get back into the motorcade after a visit) by the campaign manager and his team. If we arrived too early, the people Mum was supposed to meet might not be ready for her. If we arrived too late, her supporters might have got fed up and gone home, especially in bad weather. For communications and back-up there was a radio telephone, whose service was patchy, and the services of someone from Research, who carried two massive suitcases into which they could delve for some relevant fact or statistic about anything from NHS waiting times to the EC policy on pig-rearing.

If we arrived somewhere and the weather had turned foul, or a farmyard was muddier than expected, wellies and headscarves had to be found pronto. (Once, Mum had to borrow mine – fortunately, they fitted.) Mum was indefatigable, plunging into the melee at each new destination, waving and smiling at the sea of faces and the children hoisted on to shoulders for a better view. What I called 'Maggie and the Media Show' rolled inexorably on, with cameramen even more determined to get 'the shot of the day' than the crazed bargain hunters I'd faced at the Harrods sales.

At one supermarket Mum visited and was invited to shop in, the press walked backwards in front of her as she made her way along the aisles, endangering display pyramids of tins and packets, and threatening to demolish the whole egg stock. Some photographers balanced precariously on the edge of fish-filled freezers. I watched Mum pick up a few items and place them in her basket, and realised this kind of shopping was a novel experience for her – she probably hadn't shopped in a supermarket for several years. I foresaw that she was going to buy what she could reach, rather than what we needed at Number Ten – loo paper and instant coffee – so I whipped round the rest of the deserted aisles in record time, paid and put the box of provisions in the back of the car.

I returned for the finale – the prime minister paying at the checkout. Mum waited while her purchases were totted up: Lymeswold cheese (English, of course), a packet of ox tongue, some light bulbs, ham and pâté. Then came the hiccup. 'Carol, could you please pay?' the Iron Lady called from the middle of the crush. Ducking under boom mikes and pushing through the wall of Nikon and Canon cameras, I coughed up £11.94 and filled the carrier bag while Mum held forth on food prices, inflation and Conservative policy on consumer issues. At a hardware store further along the campaign trail, Mum decided that our home in Flood Street was in need of a new hammer and screwdriver, took them to the counter and ordered me to pay. Expensive things, these elections, I thought to myself.

Mum didn't always receive such a warm reception. There were plenty of demonstrators from the CND or anti-war lobbies waiting in the wings. She often had to shout to be heard above the jeers and boos. At one particularly noisy demonstration, her security men managed to get her inside in double-quick time, but left me floundering outside. My only choice was to sit in my locked car and endure men in Ku Klux Klan-style outfits kicking the doors, yelling 'Tory Scum Out!' and jeering menacingly at me through the windows.

The ferocious pace of the three-week campaign staggered me. Mum notched up three thousand miles, travelling to more than thirty towns and cities. There were constant photo calls – Mum at a factory, Mum on a walkabout, Mum cuddling a calf, Mum eating fish and chips. I would trail behind collecting up the bouquets she was given. Dad was there, too, at the back, chatting to those without a hope in hell of seeing Mum, or caught up in the press scrum. Feeling like a referee sometimes, he only wished he could hand out a few red cards. After one eleven-minute factory tour (which was all the time it was allotted on her schedule), he thanked the managing director and said he would come back at a quieter time to find out what they actually made.

At the Cadbury's factory in a Birmingham marginal, my

mother found herself balancing on the brink of successive vats of swirling chocolate, with the crush of photographers threatening to propel her into them at any moment. Few appreciated it at the time, but the Iron Lady narrowly missed being incorporated into a range of delicious walnut whips. The history of Britain over the next decade could have been very different.

At an aeronautics factory in Wiltshire, we were scheduled to see a demonstration of the Optica observation aircraft. Mum declined the offer of going up in a prototype of the plane. I, however, foolishly agreed to take her place. Strapped into the no-fuss cabin of this glass-bubble-fronted, buzz-box-type machine, we bumped off along the grass runway like a speeding golf buggy. It was an excellent joyride, although I wasn't sure when the pilot suggested we could see if we could do a bow like a Harrier. Looking at my watch, and ever mindful of the schedule, I realised that we were due to leave the airfield in about seven minutes and that delaying factors like crashes and rescues would undoubtedly prove unpopular, so declined. It was probably just as well: two years later the Optica crashed, killing two police officers, and the company eventually went out of business.

Wherever she went, my mother continued to work the crowd. She was alternately charming and then in thundering form, depending on what was required. One minute she'd be piercingly interested in the manufacture of a new electronic timer ('Can I use this for my rollers?'), the next there were cries of 'She's on the move!' and the press would abandon half-eaten sarnies and scramble over themselves to get back to their vehicles and follow in her wake. I had the unnerving feeling that everyone was waiting for her to make a mistake or show signs of cracking under the pressure.

On plane trips, Mum's campaign team would be furiously compiling and typing out a speech she was to deliver on landing. Even as the plane taxied to a halt, she'd be scribbling amendments and adding a word here or there. Watching her work late into the night with her speech-writers and red boxes, I marvelled at how she coped with the relentless pace of the campaign trail. I was exhausted and I was a fraction of her age. A press photographer dropped dead of a heart attack right in front of us one day. Mum was deeply distressed and somehow found the time to write to his widow.

One night, I found her in the sitting room shortly before 2 a.m. She had kicked off her shoes and tucked her feet beneath her on the sofa. Behind her hung a painting of Chequers. Before her stood a coffee table decorated with a map of the Falkland Islands, worked in wood by apprentices of the Royal Aircraft Establishment in Bedfordshire. On it stood a basket of blue flowers which I had managed to save from the crush earlier in the day. I watched her from the doorway for a minute, thinking that the job of PM is a lonely one.

Knowing she was off to Yorkshire early the next morning, I put my foot down. 'Come on now, Mum, isn't it time you went to bed? You must be exhausted.'

'I am not allowed to be,' she replied. When I saw her resistance, I insisted much more firmly.

Sighing, Mum closed and locked her completed red boxes, tidied away papers into a briefcase, picked up empty glasses and plumped up flattened cushions – anything to spin out a few more minutes. She was wide awake and far too keyed up to sleep, but I thought that at least getting her into bed would be a step in the right direction.

'Goodnight. Please try to go to sleep,' I pleaded, seeing her to her room. I felt a bit of a bully – albeit, I told myself, a righteous one.

The last few days of the campaign became increasingly frenetic and the political correspondents following my mother's trail began to complain that she wasn't giving them enough time. To make their point, they took a page out of Ronnie Millar's book and penned a song to the tune of 'Daisy, Daisy', which went like this:

Maggie, Maggie, give us an interview,
We're all crazy to have a word with you.
We don't need a lot of copy,
But Maggie, we're gonna get stroppy
If you don't, toute suite,
Get to your feet
And give us a par or two.

We had been in such a state of flux for so many weeks that we didn't know if we were coming or going. Number Ten had become like a no man's land. I had deliberately run down the contents of the freezer in case we had to make a hasty retreat. My parents usually held a party at Number Ten following the Trooping of the Colour, but – as no one knew if we would still be the incumbents the following week – we were unable to confirm anything. 'We don't count our chickens until they hatch,' Mum insisted.

At the youth rally for Young Conservatives at Wembley Conference Centre in the final week of the campaign, she showed a rare moment of stage fright. Waiting in the dimly lit wings for her cue to go on, she confided, 'Oh, how I wish it was over.'

Her reception, however, was so rapturous that it seemed the chickens had not only hatched but were laying again. The whole event resembled an American presidential rally, as two-and-a-half rapturous young voices screamed for 'Maggie!' spurred on by the likes of celebrity supporters Kenny Everett, Jimmy Tarbuck, Bob Monkhouse and assorted sports stars. After her speech, when she did a lap of honour, shaking hands in the aisles, it was like something from a Leicester Square premiere.

She left the rally to record a party political broadcast which, to my mind, was one of her finest. Speaking straight to camera, she said, 'May I suggest to every citizen of our country, every man and every woman of whatever political persuasion, that on Thursday you pause and ask yourself one question: who would be best to defend our freedom, our way of life, and the much-loved land in which we live? Britain is on the right track. Don't turn back.'

In the final few days of the campaign, I barely saw her. The only indications that she was around were the constant phone calls from the front door to tell me that the hairdresser was on his way up, or that the TV make-up girl had arrived. I just scanned her schedule, laid out the relevant changes of clothes, returned the discarded ones to their rightful cupboards or caught a glimpse of her dashing down the stairs or out of the front door.

On the last day, we found ourselves on the Isle of Wight, venue of our happiest childhood holidays, with an excitable end-of-term feeling. Even the short flight was blissful, because earlier in the campaign the journey would have been crammed with activities like amending a speech, taking in a briefing, or catching up on correspondence. Now we could all sit back and gaze down at England's green and pleasant land, while our helicopter chased its shadow across fields, down dales and over the sparkling Solent.

The press photographers clearly picked up on the mood because they donned Tory-blue T-shirts bearing the slogan: *Hilda's Personal Photographer* (Hilda, Mum's middle name, was a nickname used for her by the press, along with 'Attila the Hen'). It was a good joke and Mum happily posed with them while others snapped away. As Alistair McAlpine had said in 1979, winning is fun.

Fun it might be, but for Mum it was far from over. The strain of the campaign and the drawn-out events of that final night began to show. On the morning of polling day, she almost lost her famous cool over a missing gateau, sent as a gift from a London patisserie, with the words 'Victory Again!' iced across it. Wanting to take it to her constituency to share with her party workers if she won, she discovered that it had vanished from the kitchen in the flat and ordered an immediate search of Number Ten. Fortunately, the sixteen-inch Grand-Marnier sponge hadn't been scoffed by me or some hungry member of staff, but was safely ensconced in the cold store and was retrieved just in time.

At eleven o'clock at night it was time for us to leave Number Ten and go up to Finchley for the count. The front hall of the house looked like a stage set, illuminated by the brilliant television lights just outside the windows. I watched as she stepped into the dazzling spotlights and told the world confidently, 'I consider that this will be my home for the next five years.'

When we arrived for the count at Hendon town hall, the atmosphere was surreal, thanks to a glut of eccentric candidates who had decided to take advantage of the reduced fee for running and go up against the PM in her seat. We had Screaming Lord Sutch from the Official Monster Raving Looney Party, someone from an anti-Falklands War campaign called Belgrano Bloodhunger, another from Rail Not Motorway, a chap from the Party of Associates with Licensees who wanted to ban every licensing law (an excellent manifesto, in my opinion), a woman from the Woman/Life, Earth/Ecology Party and one truly over-the-top candidate dressed as Batman who was campaigning for

Law and Order in Gotham City. I was rather amused. My mother, I think, was mildly annoyed because all these extra candidates (one of whom demanded a recount) meant that the process took even longer than forecast.

The Belgrano Bloodhunger candidate especially upset her. There were already calls for an enquiry into the sinking of the Argentine ship and some had accused Mum of 'glorifying Falklands slaughter'. Her response was understandably emotional. 'They have the luxury of knowing we came through all right,' she told me, bitterness in her voice as she recalled that dreadful day at Chequers when she had given the order to sink it. 'I had the anxiety of protecting our people, on *Hermes* and *Invincible*, and the people on the vessels going down there.'

Knowing that the campaign was over and that the results now lay in the hands of forty-two million voters, I asked my mother why she wanted another four years in what was 'a hell of a job.' Her reply was typical: 'Because it is the job I most wanted to do in the world, and I think I've got something still to give to it.'

At about 2.20 a.m., while we were waiting in a rather stark room at the town hall for word, we watched a television newscaster inform us that the Tory party needed only fifteen more seats for victory, adding prophetically, 'Mrs Thatcher is back in Number Ten.' In exasperation, my mother shot back at the screen, 'No! I'm still at Hendon town hall!'

There had been losses and wins, but it was only when the Conservative gains started to come in thick and fast that Mum began to relax. After what seemed like an age, eventually the returning officer was ready. In a chamber full of eccentrics and exhausted party workers, my mother's majority was announced, an increase of more than fourteen hundred. Mum couldn't have looked less like a triumphant prime minister who had just won a historic victory and was heading for a substantial majority in the Commons. She looked and sounded tense, and made a very low-key vote of thanks. There was no euphoric rhetoric, just a feeling of her humility and the overwhelming responsibility that the job carried.

Diverting via Conservative Central Office at dawn to thank her staff, she eventually returned wearily to Number Ten as the sun was coming up, around four o'clock in the morning. I'd dashed back ahead of her, eager to snatch a shot of Mum coming in through the front door – a famous entry across one of the world's most famous thresholds. As well as TV lights outside, we now had them in the hall, too. Waving wildly to the world on the steps, she and Dad finally turned to come inside.

'Welcome home,' said the house manager, Peter Taylor. After 'landslide victory', these must have been the two most heart-warming words she heard that night.

'Congratulations,' I told her with a kiss. 'I'm thrilled for you.'

Upstairs, dazed but happy, Mum waved at well-wishers from a first-floor window, Dad at her side. Half an hour later, she eventually agreed to go to bed. 'I wonder if there is world news,' she said, picking up her bedside transistor radio.

'I think you'll find you're it,' I replied.

It was gone five in the morning. As I closed my mother's bedroom door I heard the radio quietly informing her that Margaret Thatcher won a second term.

Chapter Nine

WAVING,
NOT DROWNING

THERE WERE UNOPENED red boxes on the sitting-room floor crammed with voluminous files awaiting the prime minister's attention. As she sat working on the first, she had kicked her shoes off. But that was the only relaxed element. A sheaf of papers in one hand, she was on the phone.

'I want the statistics in the format I asked for, not this one,' she demanded.

Rather sympathising with whoever she was speaking to, I said, 'Bit fierce, Mum.' Silly of me. No such thing as too fierce in her repertoire.

She explained that for an answer in Prime Minister's Questions she had requested the figures compiled in a way which offered her the most potent weapon to fire at an opposition MP. And she was jolly well going to get them the way she wanted them, in order to land that knock-out blow.

Paperwork dominated our lives. There was always an avalanche of it coming in for the PM's attention and being returned with blue felt-tip Maggie amendments. To me the system looked like a hyped-up version of a college professor marking hundreds of exam papers. But for her there was never a let-up.

Whenever she was called upon to make a major speech, her contribution was to check draft after draft and scribble her amendments in the margins, right up to the eleventh hour. Often there were reminders to herself at the top of each page, like 'Relax!', 'Slow down,' or 'Lower your speaking voice.' The instructions she wrote to her staff were often completely illegible because the blue felt-tip symbols were so squashed together in the small space available. Despairing secretaries, charged with trying to decipher them and type up the next version ASAP, would say pleadingly, 'You must be able to read this, Carol, you're her *daughter*!' – as if genetics had varnished on to me some graphology dimension. I did my best but often feared that our sometimes wildly random guesses might inadvertently have changed government policy.

During Mum's time in office, friends were often amazed when I told them how tension levels rocketed in the corridors of power when some speech or other was in the process of being written. Didn't a speechwriter just hand her a copy of her speech a moment before she advanced to the podium, much as an actor might be presented with a script? I laughed. Not in the Thatcher household.

In A *Thousand Days*, Arthur Schlesinger Jnr's biography of John F. Kennedy, he described the late president's speechwriting process:

> He handed both drafts to me and issued the classic presidential injunction: 'Weave them together. Ted and I protested mildly that they were two different speeches. The President got up and headed towards the bedroom for his nap. 'I think you fellows have enough to go on,' he said. 'Just go out and write it up and have a new draft here by five o'clock.'

My mother had two methods of speechwriting. The quicker and easier, employed towards the end of a meal, was when she would whip a piece of paper out of her handbag, pen a few key phrases on it, and then ad lib the rest. The other was protracted, tortuous and absolutely agonising for everyone involved. In her memoir *The Path to Power*, she wrote of the peculiar challenge of a major speech – no matter how experienced the speaker:

> The Leader's speech at a Party Conference is quite unlike the Conference speeches of other front-bench spokesmen. It has to cover a sufficiently wide number of subjects to avoid the criticism that one has 'left out' some burning issue. Yet each

section of the speech has to have a thematic correspondence with all the other sections. Otherwise, you finish up with what I used to call a 'Christmas tree', on which pledges and achievements are hung and where each new topic is classically announced by the mind-numbing phrase 'I now turn to . . .'. A powerful speech of the sort required to inspire the Party faithful, as well as easing the worries of the doubters, is in some ways more like a piece of poetry than prose. No one should be tempted to use flowery language, but rather [ensure] that it is the ideas, sentiments and mood below the surface which count.

When my mother gave her first speech as prime minister to the annual Tory party conference, my father wrote the following account of the fraught countdown to the completed text in a letter to me:

Going backwards over the last few weeks, I start with the PM's speech to the Conference yesterday. The drafting was a nightmare: the worst long night of all the Conference speeches. We went to bed at 6.10 a.m. and it was not finished. On again at 10.00 a.m., the final sheets were completed around 1.00 p.m. to stand up at 2.15 p.m.! In the event it was a very fine speech and extremely well received by this morning's press and I would confidently expect a good press in tomorrow's Sundays.

I once asked my mother why she liked to have so much input in her speeches and didn't just leave it to the writers, as some prime ministers did. She was quite indignant. 'Oh, it's got to be my ideas,' she replied. 'Not every bit of the draft is mine, as you know, but I go through it all. First we do the ideas, then they go away and draft, then that draft's usually torn up, then we do another one and then I literally spend hours and hours going through that. We change it and change it, and some speeches we'd still be changing now, if we hadn't delivered them already.' She admitted that she often reached a podium wishing she could tear the speech up and start again, and preferred to speak off the cuff on the hustings, coming up with three key ideas and sticking to them.

My tiny contribution to this infernal process was to provide refreshments, especially when speechwriters were summoned to the flat at Number Ten for working dinners. Some didn't disguise their dismay at the prospect of the limited menu. Ronnie Millar wrote, '[These suppers] *invariably consisted of coronation chicken or shepherd's pie, coronation chicken or lasagne, coronation chicken or boeuf stroganoff.*' Early on in my mother's political career it was blindingly obvious that speechwriting, or indeed any paperwork, would be attacked with fierce concentration, and anything more mundane – like domesticity – almost entirely forgotten.

Another evening, one of the writers was taking his time over his scratch Sunday supper ~~supper~~ and my mother's impatience was palpable. I gave him a nudge and advised him to polish it off pronto, as the PM was desperate to get back to work. He'd hardly put down his knife and fork before my mother pressed the 'Eject' button on her government-issue dining chair and proclaimed, 'Let's get back and have a go at that section on the trade unions.' With that she was off, turning right up the three steps, left along the main corridor and down to the sitting room – her wordsmiths in her slipstream.

A precedent had been set for speech dramas in Edinburgh during the 1979 election campaign, in an episode which was etched on the memories of all who were there. Mum, preparing to address a rally at Leith town hall, was in a last-minute frazzle. Five minutes after she should have left, having only just taken the curlers out of her hair, she was found with scissors and paste in hand, cutting and gluing sections of the speech together on the floor in an against-the-clock rehash. Arrows and unintelligible notes pointed the way to the next sentence, and the script began to resemble some art student's collage. The net result was that several of the pages got stuck together as the light on the lectern dried out the glue. This not only shortened Mum's performance but didn't exactly aid smooth continuity.

Even after a speech which had gone down well, Mum never paused to soak up the success, as the letters of thanks she wrote to Ronnie Millar indicate. This one was after the 1977 party conference:

Dear Ronnie,

How can I thank you for helping? The short answer is that I

An early photo-call
for the political twins
(co-starring the teddy)

A daughterly scowl –
not impressed with Ma's
version of Chopsticks

Like father like daughter. I'm sure Dad had a G and T in hand too

Boxes from Number Ten: Mum's idea of relaxation

1983 – behind the leader on the campaign trail

Shoes off and papers everywhere – an informal moment at Chequers

A long way from Pommy politics on a beach in Bondi

1977 – Mum and me
in oversized shades
on the Great Wall
of China

The First Lady of Russia
looks on surprised at
Iron Lady Junior's prattle

PROGRAMME
FOR THE
VISIT
OF
THE RT HON MARGARET THATCHER MP
PRIME MINISTER OF GREAT BRITAIN
AND NORTHERN IRELAND
AND MR. DENIS THATCHER, MBE
TO
BOMBAY

Friday, the 17th April 1981
to
Sunday, the 19th April 1981

Chequers

Monday, 7th May 1990

Avocado Pear with Lobster
Chablis Domaine Jean Durup, 1986

Rack of Lamb
Minted New Potatoes
Garden Vegetables
Château Talbot, 19

Lemon Soufflé

Cheese Beignets
with Mint and Apple Chutney
Graham,

The President of the United States
and Mrs. Reagan
will greet
The Right Honorable
The Prime Minister of the United
Kingdom of Great Britain and
Northern Ireland
and Mr. Thatcher

10.00 a.m., Thursday
February 26, 1981
at the White House

A new year and the politics are someone else's problem

Cheers!

Dad's eightieth birthday cake iced with himself on the cover of *Private Eye*

Careful! Don't strangle the *Spitting Image* puppet of your own mother!

Birdlife in
the Falklands

2006 – my centre-court tennis commentary in the royal box

Bushtucker Trial – I prefer taxis

My crowning moment

A year on – the last days of my Aussie reign on the Australian surf

Trying to live up to Jungle Queen glamour

can't. As usual you were magnificent throughout the week at Blackpool and without you everything would not have fallen into place so smoothly. Your humour, patience and professionalism is always a source of great encouragement to me and I will never forget what you have done.

With best wishes,

Then, in her own hand, she added, 'I just don't know <u>how</u> we shall do better next year. Lots of love, Margaret.'

Speechwriters were always on the treadmill. In another letter to Ronnie, in 1989, she wrote,

I should like to thank you, as always, for your enormous help with my speech to the Scottish Party Conference last week. It was very good of you to give up so much time, and your contribution was invaluable. Indeed, it was widely remarked that the humour contained within the speech played a major part in its success. I very much hope you will be able to help us with the Women's Speech, which I am afraid is all too soon, and I know John Whittingdale will be contacting you about this shortly . . .

Ronnie said later that anyone who participated in Mum's annual party conference speech – which was a killer – was hooked for life . . . 'Or what remained of it.' He went on, 'There was something compulsive about the agony, the despair and lack of sleep, the sheer impossibility that a coherent sequence of words and thoughts and images and policies could ever emerge, the excitement when a faint glimmer of hope appeared on the horizon, and finally the lady's inevitable triumph.'

As a rule, my mother's sense of humour was best suited to rapid-fire repartee from the despatch box. She didn't really 'do' jokes and, while she could laugh at many, sometimes didn't 'get' them.

During the marathon writing of one conference speech, she was very uptight and confided to Ronnie, 'I wish it was over!'

Reassuring her, he tried to instil confidence by saying, 'Piece of cake.'

'Good heavens! Not now!' came the sharp reply.

It was Dad who could always make her see sense. Before her triumphant address to the party conference in Blackpool in 1975 (her first), the speech had gone through umpteen drafts in the Thatcher suite at the Imperial Hotel, a process which stopped only when my exhausted father interjected and cried: 'That's the one!'

In the car on the way to the conference, Dad held her hand to stop it shaking. On the platform, standing in front of five thousand people, she pinned her arms to her sides for the same reason. Then she launched into the speech that had caused so many headaches for so long. 'Our leaders have been different men with different qualities and different styles, but they all had one thing in common – each met with the challenge of his time . . . What are our chances of success? It depends on what kind of people we are. What kind of people are we? We are the people who have received more Nobel prizes than any other nation except America.'

As cries of 'Hear! Hear!' rang out (led by Dad), she added: 'We are also the people who, among other things, invented the computer, the refrigerator, the electric motor, the stethoscope, rayon, the steam turbine, stainless steel, television, penicillin, radar, the jet engine, hovercraft, carbon fibres and the best half of the Concorde.'

When the speech was over, Mum acknowledged the uproarious applause and then returned to her hotel suite, where everyone was on a high. Ronnie Millar congratulated her and told her that – as he'd just spoken to the press – he had it on impeccable authority that she would receive rave reviews.

Mum's reaction was typically low-key. 'Well, if they're right,' she said cautiously, 'what are we going to do next year? Brighton could be the most dreadful anti-climax.'

Dad, sitting on the sidelines, erupted, 'My God, woman, you've just had a bloody great triumph and here you are worrying yourself sick about next year! I'll get the others, shall I? Then you can settle down for another all-night session. I mean, obviously there's no time to be lost . . .'

Besides the speeches, there were drafts of the election manifesto, policy initiatives, newspaper articles under her by-line and correspondence to be tackled. The letters of condolence she wrote to the families of soldiers killed in action, and to many other victims of tragedy, genuinely moved her. I recall one sunny afternoon at Chequers when I saw her looking sombre and very absorbed. When I asked if anything was wrong, she emerged from her thoughts and told me she was struggling with how to offer some solace to the widow of a policeman who had been gunned down.

About the only writing Mum didn't do was to keep a diary. I guess her memory was always so formidable that she either didn't feel the need, or viewed such an occupation as an extravagant waste of time.

But she did keep a diary of sorts – in her letters to me. In the era before texts, e-mails, mobile phones and instant news, it was not easy to keep in touch, especially during my four years in Australia, but I could not have had a more conscientious political correspondent than my mother. During her final years as leader of the opposition and her first year as prime minister, she somehow conjured up the time to write long, newsy letters telling me all about what was going on. These welcome missives dropped into my mailbox in Sydney, providing an extraordinary insight into her unique perspective on life. Detailed, entertaining and utterly riveting, they would often start: '*For a few moments, I have a pause in a busy week . . .*' and then go on for six pages.

I mislaid this correspondence for decades until clearing out an old filing cabinet. Rereading the bundle of blue airmail letters, I marvelled at the combination of my mother's concern for a daughter far away, mingled with her own take on the political inside track, and peppered with more mundane family news. She would talk of major decisions she needed to make with absolute clarity; insights that were a privilege to read and to have. Many of my contemporary journalists with a beat in politics would have killed to have been on the receiving end of such correspondence.

30th October 1977

Dear Carol-Jane,

Daddy is enquiring this week about an American Express card for you. We understand you can use it there and we can pay in sterling here up to certain amounts.

We read here that Malcolm Fraser [then the Liberal Party Prime Minister of Australia] has decided to have an election on December 10. I do hope he hasn't made a mistake – but he is the best judge of his own political circumstances. It just seems as if you have a lot of General Elections over there. Over here we could do with one, but as yet, I see no sign. The recent budget [Labour] was a bit oversold and people thought they were going to get more out of it than they did.

Mark is at home doing a pre-dash study course before another finals course [accountancy]. I just hope he makes it this time because I am convinced he must have a qualification. We are down at Scotney this weekend but after today I haven't another free weekend before Christmas. I just hope that dashing about the country and the world does some good.

I haven't got many trips in the offing yet. The Shah has asked me to visit Iran sometime in 1978 and I shall have to go . . . we could drift on for another two years without an election and if we do we shall have to play the hand as best we can.

Daddy and I went up to Crown Derby factory to buy the office etc Christmas gifts. The chairman was there so I got a staff discount! Thank goodness because the prices had gone up quite a lot.

I don't know yet what re-shuffling to do among the number two in shadow. A few changes need to be made. Bringing them in is not the difficulty. It is who to put out that causes the problems. Somehow I shall have to strengthen the financial team. Brain power is not good enough. You need personality and impact as well.

Another came after my mother had given a television interview to Granada's *World in Action* programme in January 1978. Her comment that British people feared they might be 'rather swamped by people with a different culture' had ignited the immigration debate. She went on to say, 'The British character has done so much for democracy, for law, and done so much throughout the world that if there is any fear that it might be swamped people are going to react and be rather hostile to those coming in.' This is how Mum described the furore to me at the time:

My dear Carol,

I seem to have come through a battering these last few weeks. It all started with laryngitis but as there was no possibility of time off I just had to carry on and it had to come at a particularly busy time. I had some radio and television interviews to do. As events happened, they asked questions about immigration which I answered in my usual straight-forward way - but the commentators haven't stopped talking about it for three whole weeks!

The Labour party have called me everything under the sun but we have had about ten thousand letters (extra) - all of them, save a handful, in fervent support.

Ted Heath said I hadn't got it right and Enoch Powell said I hadn't got it right so I must have got it about right if they are both disgruntled!

The next day I did the Jimmy Young Show, which I thoroughly enjoyed.

We are still struggling to get Central Office right. We have appointed Gordon [Reece] Head of Publicity - at least Gordon is an optimist and an enthusiast and has lots of ideas. He will drop a few clangers but so does anyone who does something. If only I knew when the election would be I should know when to reshuffle but it may not be until next year, although things do seem a bit restless at the moment.

What else have we done? I had to speak at a lunch in the City to overseas bankers – about two hundred of them. It was a little heavy-going but then their sense of humour isn't like ours. I also spoke to about four hundred London bankers at a dinner in the City. They were easier because we all understood the same things.

Mark has gone to Paris this weekend – a kind of last fling before serious sales work. He hasn't come in yet although it is 10.55pm and I don't know whether he will return tonight or tomorrow morning. There is an envelope downstairs which I don't like to open. It contains the result of his exams which I fear will be a bitter disappointment.

Next week is much quieter but I expect attacks on us will materialise. Gordon heard one of the Daily Mirror reporters at a press conference saying, 'We have got to stop this woman! I thought it was quite a compliment!

She was stoical about the extension to her time as leader of the opposition, but she was thoroughly honest in the next 'bluey' letter she penned to me with its distinctive House of Commons postmark:

Darling Carol,
Now, we face quite a long haul. I feel sure that the PM will

not think of an election before May [1979] at the earliest and not then unless he thinks he is going to win. Moreover I can't see the minor parties all joining with us to vote him down. The prospect of having to keep up everyone's morale with a year to go is not an easy one but at least we know we have only one year to wait and things can't go on after that.

I just hope the conference goes well next week – but anything can happen.

I come on [to speak] on Friday afternoon this year. The whole week to wait! Will write soon after the Brighton Conference.

Lots of Love

Mummy xx

When she did finally become prime minister, the first substantial challenge on the foreign-affairs front was to find a solution for the situation in Rhodesia (as Zimbabwe was called then). Ever since Ian Smith had declared independence from Britain in 1965, sparking the Rhodesian Bush War and the end of white-minority rule, the country and its future had posed a problem for successive British governments. It was still in a state of civil war; a route to peace and security had to be found.

In 1979, the Commonwealth Heads of Government Meeting (CHOGM) was held in Lusaka, Zambia, the first time it had been held in Africa.

Later, I enjoyed comparing contemporary newspaper reports

with Mum's account of the summit – a marvellous insight into the rather unconventional nitty-gritty of diplomacy:

My darling Carol,

I promised I would write to you about the saga of Lusaka, Zambia. We arrived . . . at 10.25pm. It was dark but a blaze of lights from TV cameras greeted us.

There must have been three to four hundred press-men and cameras there. They were uncontrollable and surrounded myself and the official greeting party. The only thing was to smile one's way through. Eventually we reached the V.I.P. lounge where the Zambian PM, Daniel Lisulo, and I were ushered into a small room wholly separated from the rest of my party. The doors had been slammed firmly on everyone else. I wondered why, but was soon to know. Within a minute or two a message came that the next room was 'ready'. The PM and I went in and there was the entire Zambian press – radio and TV – all set up for a press conference. Again no discipline; they just clustered round shouting questions. It was a complete set-up. I. is as well one is used to such things and can keep one's cool.

As CHOGM progressed there was a very nervous frisson that the contents of the joint communiqué – and what had been agreed for the solution of Rhodesia – had been leaked. The storm broke on Sunday evening during a church service. I had to go to the cathedral (in Lusaka) for a special

Commonwealth service and to read the second lesson. [Kenneth] Kaunda [president of Zambia] was there and the Secretary-General of the Commonwealth [Mr Shridath Ramphal] was reading the first lesson. During the service, a note was sent up to me confirming what had happened [the leak]. I passed it to the Secretary-General and then read my lesson!

The *Daily Telegraph* the next day informed me that the lesson she read was John 15: 12–17:

This is my commandment, that you love one another as I have loved you. No one has greater love than this, to lay down one's life for one's friends. You are my friends if you do what I command you. I do not call you servants any longer, because the servant does not know what the master is doing; but I have called you friends, because I have made known to you everything that I have heard from my Father.

During the sermon that followed, Mum was subjected to a political harangue from the pulpit. The Archbishop repeated 'God is a racist' three times. My Ma filled me in: '*After that, the sermon. Another vitriolic occasion. The Roman Catholic Archbishop of Zambia [Milingo] spoke of everything except Christianity. The Secretary-General and I agreed there was more*

Christianity in the conference than in the cathedral that day. Of course, most of the Archbishop's remarks were aimed at Britain and therefore at me.'

The *Telegraph* claimed: 'Mrs Thatcher, in cream dress and large navy hat looked at her cream shoes.' According to my mother, far from admiring her footwear, she was in overdrive.

My mind was elsewhere. We had too many chestnuts to pull out of the fire to bother about what was being said from the pulpit. The Secretary-General and I, by means of notes passed between us during the rest of the service, agreed the only thing to do was to get all heads of government together for a meeting at a party being given that night ... by Malcolm Fraser. I left the cathedral with as much outward composure as I could muster. We agreed to go straight to the Frasers' where most PMs (not having been to church) were already engaged in jollifications.

We were all packed together in a small room for fifty minutes of the most nerve-racking meeting I have ever attended. Most people were very angry that the thing had been leaked before they ever knew about it. At times during those fifty minutes I thought we should lose everything as they tried to unpack the carefully agreed package. Eventually however with help ... we won through and the thing was published intact.

This achieved, the end of the conference lightened up with the *Daily Telegraph* observing, 'Mrs Thatcher, who arrived in Lusaka with an image that would have embarrassed a gorgon left as Zambia's Number One sweetheart – "Maggie" to all and sundry.'

Mum was perceptive enough to recognise this as only the beginning and her letter continued: *'Now the difficult work begins . . . There are so many rapids to be negotiated it will be a miracle if we come through. But we really must strain every sinew to do it. For Rhodesia's sake.'*

The final paragraph proved what a reluctant holidaymaker she was.

Daddy and I go to Islay on Wednesday. It will be a change – but I would almost rather stay here and get on . . . Daddy came home on Saturday having been in the Midlands on business. Incidentally, he opened a charity cricket match last Sunday bowling the first ball and he clean bowled the batsman! He will be in great demand to open a Test match next. He is also undertaking quite a programme of public engagements, especially in the sporting world, and doing them very well. We await more news of you eagerly. Next week is Lord Mountbatten's funeral – a sad ceremonial indeed, then Balmoral for the weekend, then back for the Rhodesian talks.

Lots of love

Mummy xx

As I reread all these letters, my mind boggled at the way my mother wrote a few paragraphs wearing her prime ministerial hat and then continued in Mum-mode.

Her 1980 Christmas letter on Downing Street notepaper is a good example:

Darling Carol,

Here is the second part of your Christmas present. Alas we still haven't been able to get nice earrings for pierced ears. I don't know what kind of Christmas it will be for us. You remember that last year 'Afghanistan' happened on Boxing Day. This year we keep a watchful eye on Poland but at home we have the hunger strike in the Maze Prison and it looks as if those on it are going to continue until death – and that would be about Christmas time. Our fear is that those deaths would cause violence and strife on the streets in Northern Ireland.

The next six months will be difficult politically especially with rising unemployment but we shall have to ride the storm. Economically things will get better before the unemployment figures fall.

Lots of love – will phone you over Xmas.

Mummy xx

Some letters were spread over several weeks, especially when foreign affairs intervened:

Chancellor Schmidt came over on a private visit a few days ago and we had a long talk. Contrary to what the press said the talks went rather well but I fear we are not getting very far with our budget problem. All the other nations are trying to shelve it and are hoping we shall be generous and understanding of their problems, as we usually are. But it is time for them to understand ours. We have been generous for too long and got precious little thanks in recognition for it.

A week later the letter was still not completed.

We have finished Cabinet early for once and I am determined to get this letter off however incomplete. This week has been busy in the sense that, in addition to everything else, I had to do an interview for French TV . . . The [European] budget question is now assuming enormous proportions and France is making difficult statements. I fear we shall have another very nasty session at the summit in Brussels.

This evening after Questions in the House, I am going up to Yorkshire for a tour. We are going to the new Selby coal mine, if we can get in. News has reached us that Scargill is organising a mass picket of miners and steelworkers to try to prevent me from getting in! Just to add to our problems, one of the firms I was due to visit chose this week to make one hundred and fifty research workers redundant and they now have a real problem on their hands with the unions! Not a very nice prospect but we just have to go through with it.

Will phone on Sunday. Have received your letters . . .

Lots of love

Mummy xx

Dad wrote, too, though never so fulsomely, or so often. Usually, it was to sprinkle some personal news with his opinion on the government's fortunes. One started:

Nearly six months now since the Election and the Government is getting, in general, a good press. The reduction in the massive increases in Public Expenditure planned by the Socialists is and will cause trouble, and one does detect an underlying fear in the minds of a large number of people that we are in for a winter of savage union strife. If we could introduce some measures to make strikes expensive for strikers, in time some of the difficulties might or could be avoided.

Some criticism has been made of the Prime Minister's 'style'. We all know she is brisk and determined, but leaks in Whitehall from Cabinet Ministers (amongst others) to the press accuse her of being 'dictatorial'; this is clearly unfair. She has been rather hurt by this. I have tried to say "ignore it" but "remember not everyone can comprehend difficult problems and is able to think as fast as you can."

Outside of the job, the main problem is to get your Mother to relax. She enjoys it here [Chequers] but works ninety per cent of the time. . . Just where we go for a holiday in the future – having regard to the needs of security and having [at least one member of Downing Street staff] as a minimum always available – is an extremely difficult problem. So far I have not come up with a glimmer of an answer . . .

Unlike your Mother I have had a holiday. Last week I spent eight days in Portugal with Bill Deedes and two others playing golf in super weather. Twenty-seven holes a day for eight days nearly creased me. We calculated we walked nearly a hundred miles in the week!

The one subject neither of my parents touched upon in letters to me was the events of the night of 12 October 1984. I was abroad at the time, three weeks into an assignment in South Korea for the *Daily Telegraph*, when I called Number Ten to leave a message for my mother. It was to wish her a happy fifty-ninth birthday for the following day and to wish her luck in her speech at the party conference. I got through to Caroline in the Private Office.

'I am sorry to give you bad news when you are so far away,' she said, 'but there's been a bomb in Brighton. Both your parents are all right, and your mother is going to give her speech at the conference this morning.' But she told me that Norman Tebbit and his wife had been seriously injured in the explosion, which had torn the heart out of the Grand Hotel, and that several people had been killed.

Unable to change my ticket, I had to stick to my itinerary and fly back on Sunday morning. By the time I arrived at Heathrow, I felt as if I was the only person who didn't know, minute by minute, what had happened. I drove straight to Chequers, where Mum had just returned from church. I found her on the terrace and she was still shaken. 'This is the day I was not meant to see,' she told me. Dad, too, was quieter, more subdued. This was the only time during the Number Ten years that he didn't reply personally to the letters he received from friends and well-wishers. He had a letter of thanks printed instead; it included the line, 'I like to think God had a hand in it.' He bought Mum a watch with a rare note which read, 'Every minute is precious.'

On the night of the bombing, my mother had been in her suite working on her conference speech at about 2.50 a.m. while Dad was asleep in the adjoining bedroom. Robin Butler, her principal private secretary, was with her and wrote: 'A large thud shook the room and, after a few seconds' silence, another blast. Plaster fell from the ceiling. I knew it was a bomb. I thought a car had exploded outside; I didn't realise the bomb was actually above us. Glass from the window was strewn over the carpet and part of the ceiling collapsed. Before I could stop her, she said, "I must see if Denis is all right." She opened the door and plunged into the gloom. By now, the sound of falling masonry was deafening. To my great relief, after a few minutes she came out and Denis appeared. It touched me because it was one of those moments where there could be no play-acting and her first thought was, "I must make sure Denis isn't buried," not knowing what might have been happening in that room.'

Through clouds of cement dust, Mum then went to check on her secretarial staff in the bedroom opposite hers. One had received a shock from her electric typewriter, the other – seeing my mother – jumped up and told her, 'I've got the speech, Mrs Thatcher. It's all right. I've still got the speech. I'm just typing it.'

Mum did write down her memories of that dreadful night some time later, revealing that one fact which played on her mind afterwards was the need to keep a torch by her bed at all times, which she always did from then on. Having been led to safety through a rear entrance by her detectives and transferred to Lewes Police College for the rest of the night, while paramedics and police sifted through the wreckage, Mum was determined that the conference would go on. The police advised that she return to the safer surroundings of London but she refused.

In her temporary lodgings, Mum couldn't sleep and was at a loss as to what to do. She wrote: 'I could only think of one thing . . . Crawfie and I knelt by the side of our beds for some time in silence.' She slept fitfully for only an hour or so, fully clothed, and then woke early to watch the television news. 'The news was bad, much worse than I had feared. I saw pictures of Norman Tebbit being pulled from the rubble. Then came the news that Roberta Wakeham [wife of John] and Anthony Berry, MP, were dead. I knew that I could not afford to let my emotions get control of me. I had to be mentally and physically fit for the day ahead. I tried not to watch the harrowing pictures. But it did not seem to do much good . . .'

At 9.30 on the morning of her birthday, she walked onto the platform at the conference hall in Brighton to a colossal ovation. She told delegates that the bombing had been 'an attempt not only to disrupt and terminate our conference, it was an attempt to cripple Her Majesty's democratically elected government. That is the scale of the outrage we have all shared. And the fact that we are gathered here now, shocked but composed and determined, is a sign not only that this attack has failed, but that all attempts to destroy democracy by terrorism will fail.'

When she finished, she went straight to the local hospital to visit the injured. Four people had died, others would follow. John Wakeham was critical and in surgery, and Norman Tebbit's wife, Margaret, was paralysed from the neck down. My mother returned to Chequers that night unable to stop thinking about those who couldn't return to their homes.

The events of that night haunted us as a family for many years. I couldn't stop thinking what a close shave it had been. My mother quite rightly made us focus on those who had been more seriously affected. When Norman Tebbit was well enough to leave hospital, and his wife had been transferred to Stoke Mandeville Hospital in

Aylesbury, Mum arranged for Norman to move into Chequers, where he could be waited on hand and foot, and be close to the hospital to visit his wife. I remember seeing him there at weekends as he came to terms with what had happened.

Some years later, my mother suffered another blow. Ian Gow, MP, her close friend and former parliamentary private secretary, was killed by an IRA bomb as he started his car in the drive of his house. My mother described his loss as 'irreplaceable' and wrote: 'The loss of a friend or family member by violence leaves an even deeper scar . . .'

Chapter Ten

SWIMMING FOR
MY SUPPER

Being the recipient of second-hand fame – as I called the phenomenon, because I wasn't famous but my mother was – has its ups and downs. Some doors open, and some close. Others slam shut.

It can be a no-win situation, though in theory it looks like a win–win one. If you do well, the cynics will probably say, 'Well, with a prime minister for a mother, and all those contacts and string-pulling, how could she fail?' And if you put one foot wrong, the tabloids will pounce, eager to expose your indiscretion with sensationalism and glee. Ask my brother.

To many people, I wasn't really an individual so much as an adjunct of my mother. When I made a reservation in a restaurant, or booked a minicab, using my surname, the response might be: 'As in Maggie?' or 'Any relation?' Even my appearance was judged in relation to her. If I looked scruffy, people said, 'Such a pity she didn't inherit her mother's good looks and immaculate dress sense.' If I made an effort, and looked presentable or better, I got no credit for it: 'Well, with her connections she probably gets loads of free designer stuff.'

To other people, I was unreal. On one occasion a woman at the call centre of a credit card company scampered off to tell her supervisor they had a nutter on the line who thought her mother was prime minister.

Sometimes my fellow mortals' perception of what it was like being the PM's daughter absolutely staggered me. One friend astonished me by asking, over a glass of wine in my terraced house in Fulham, 'Do you pay rates?'

'Where do you think we are?' I shot back. 'In a banana republic?' I astonished her right back by offering to dig out the paperwork to prove that I not only paid rates but had a bog-standard mortage. No favours done by either the council or the building society.

Then there's the quandary of who and what you are trying to be. Is it a compliment or an insult when, halfway through dinner, your date says, 'Really, you're quite normal and ordinary.' Fellow journalists – not unreasonably, I suppose – assumed I must have an inside track, and implied I ought to play a role not unlike Deep Throat's in the Watergate affair. But I was mindful of Mum's threat that if I ever leaked so much as a sentence from the conversation over a weekend lunch at Chequers I'd never be invited to Sunday roast again.

My father warned me that eternal vigilance was required, but I did get tripped up occasionally. When my mother and Mrs Gandhi were addressing a session of the Indian parliament in Delhi, a photo of me appeared in a tabloid newspaper over a caption claiming that I'd fallen asleep during Mum's speech. Not true, of course. I'd had a copy of her speech on my lap, had been following the text as she spoke. But eyelids lowered equalled snoozing; caught out!

My connection with my mother certainly wasn't always advantageous. Some newspapers were happy to have me write for them, but reluctant to print my by-line. Perhaps secretly keen to get on side by joining their ranks, my real hope as a fully paid-up 'reptile' was that working in newspapers would give me the opportunity to carry on travelling to far-flung places and meeting interesting people. In that regard, my career choice certainly hasn't disappointed, and it has been especially interesting to compare my 'before and after' moments, the 'before' part being travelling with the PM and all that that entails, and the 'after' being me on my own with just a notepad and pen.

More than thirty years after my first visit to Japan with Mum, for example, I was back there in a journalistic capacity. This time, instead of the state banquets and grand apartments we stayed in, it was the hotel toilet that captivated me.

Maybe it's something in the Thatcher genes (on the paternal side) because I recall Dad once visiting a Cairo waste-water project with Mum, who was doing the honours and cutting the ribbon. He became completely engrossed by the mechanics of the system, quizzing engineers and others with a cross-examiner's zeal. For months afterwards he bored guests over Sunday lunch at Chequers with how amazing the system was, enthusing about how a London bus (double-decker, not the bendy variety) could get through the widest part of the main pipe. I think a few guests must have felt that this wasn't an entirely appropriate topic of luncheon conversation for the prime minister's weekend – particularly when there was quite enough political shit flying around the corridors of power.

For me, though, foreign sewage systems held a different fascination. Rather jetlagged and in the middle of the night in my Japanese hotel bedroom, I perused the 'Important Safeguards' printed on the underside of the lid of my Toto toilet, model number TCF 523. '*To avoid low temperature burn, turn off the warm seat when this product is used by the very young or the elderly or those who are incapacitated.*' The control panel alongside the seat featured a line of buttons, including one which played musical flushing sounds whenever I used the toilet. The others directed bottom-washing sprays from the integrated bidet that pulsed or massaged, regulated the temperature and direction of said sprays, and activated the blow-drying mechanism before the toilet flushed itself and sprayed air freshener.

Toto has sold more than twenty million toilets worldwide and has up to two hundred researchers working on new models and accessories – some for 'upper income users'. The company makes the most advanced toilets of its kind in the world, including the Washlet Zoe, which is listed in the *Guinness Book of Records* for having the most functions. Beginning to share Dad's fascination, I found myself at a Toto showroom in the city of Nagoya (home of these state-of-the-art loos), hanging off every word of a salesman who was explaining the dazzling features of the next generation of Toto toilets. I particularly liked the device that lifted the lid when it sensed a user approaching, and the disco model that came with an iPod-compatible chip. Apparently, classical music by Felix Mendelssohn is considered the most effective at relaxing the sphincter. By the end of the visit my admiration for Toto was right up there with Dad's respect for the Egyptian project.

Travelling to Kyoto, a city with an image of surreal calm, candy-floss-pink cherry blossom blooming in spring, I was looking forward to its restful Zen gardens, temples and geisha-lookalikes performing the Green Tea ceremony in which the tea is whisked to a froth. The reality was quite different. When American astronaut John Glenn arrived by bullet train – his previous travels having been as the third American to go into space and the first to orbit the Earth – he was reluctant to disembark because he didn't believe it was the Kyoto he had read about in the Japanese Tourist Board literature.

When my train drew into the same station some years later, I could see why. The terminus, built in 1997, is half a kilometre long, with at least thirty platforms, plus shopping malls, escalators and stairs linking the fifteen storeys which seem to go on for ever and have been dubbed 'Stairways to Heaven'. Fortunately, the pace was way less frenetic and futuristic when I checked into my charming *ryokan* – a traditional Japanese inn with tatami mats and sliding doors made of rice panels.

Instructed to leave my shoes at the door, I was provided with slippers throughout, including a change when I went to the bathroom. The bath was quite a novelty in itself: a tea chest in which you immersed yourself. The only drawback was that bathroom rules stated no soap except in the shower. What was impressive and a trifle mystifying, was that the tea chest was filled with hot water at night and the water was still hot the following morning. I never did find out why.

The *ryokan* was a novel experience which involved quite a lot of sitting either on the floor or on very low stools. I thus discovered that the most comfortable place to read my copy of the English-language newspaper, the *Japan Times*, was on my heated loo seat.

I am a useless linguist, so much of the fun I derive from travelling comes from working out what someone is saying to me and trying to make myself understood. When there was a knock on the door of my *ryokan* the morning I was to depart, I opened it to find a rather petite lady in a kimono. 'Karaoke?' she asked. Surely not at ten in the morning, I thought, unless it's traditional for departing guests to have a go at singing along to 'Hi, Ho, Silver Lining'? After all, the Japanese had invented karaoke back in the 1970s for those with performing aspirations. The boom had spread worldwide, and by the beginning of this century the Americans were forking out something in the region of two hundred million dollars on karaoke equipment alone.

The penny finally dropped when the kimono-clad member of staff parked her hands on the handle of my suitcase and repeated what she had said. 'Carry, OK?' My embarrassment at the misunderstanding was followed by a wave of guilt at the sight of someone half my size lugging my suitcase down to reception.

In 1981, I accompanied my mother to India when she visited Prime Minister Indira Gandhi in the country's capital, New Delhi (the trip when I 'fell asleep' during Mum's speech). As one of the prime minister's party, I was invited to stay in the president of India's official residence, a massive pile named Rashtrapati Bhevan in the heart of what is known as 'Lutyens' Delhi' after the British architect Edwin Lutyens, who designed a number of public buildings in the city. Formerly known as the Viceroy's Palace, 'Rashtrapati Bhevan' means 'Presidential Palace' in Sanskrit, and it is an appropriate title for a building impressive both in scale and in decor. In fact, it's the largest residence of any president in the world, and boasts a dome, some three hundred and forty rooms, a two-ton chandelier in one of the halls which hangs from a height of thirty-three metres, and myriad courtyards, some featuring marble lions spouting jets of water.

Late one night, one of my mother's protection officers (an unshockable, good-humoured species) was mildly surprised by an offer from one of the Indian staff. 'You like Betty?' he was asked. Mulling over whether he was being asked if he fancied the company of some Bollywood lovely for the night, he waited for more clues and finally twigged what the man was saying. It wasn't Betty he was being offered but 'bed tea'. Translation: Did he care for an early morning cuppa? Not quite the same thing.

Mrs Gandhi hosted a dinner for us in her house, and I was seated next to her charming son Rajiv, who was thirty six years-old, good-looking and softly spoken. We chatted away and as I looked across to our mothers – both Iron Ladies in their own way – I remarked to him, 'I would never go into politics. Would you?'

'No, I'm quite happy flying planes,' said Rajiv, who was then a full-time professional pilot for the country's national airline, Indian Airlines. His brother Sanjay, unquestionably the more political of Indira's sons, had been killed in an air crash the previous year and Rajiv had been elected only a couple of months before to Sanjay's parliamentary seat, but still he didn't seem very keen.

Within three years his mother had been gunned down by her Sikh bodyguards and he had stepped into her shoes, becoming India's youngest prime minister, at the age of forty. I remember talking to my mother at Chequers about Mrs Gandhi's death the day she was killed. I was wearing a simple silver rope necklace Mrs

Gandhi had given me. Although they had many political differences, my mother respected and admired the other female leader on the world stage at that time and, on her return to India some time later, she laid a wreath at the site of her funeral pyre. We spoke gloomily of the riots engulfing India in the wake of her assassination.

Seven years later, Rajiv, too, was assassinated, in Sriperumbudur by a bomb concealed in a basket of flowers and carried by a suicide bomber. His Italian widow, Sonia, became the leader of the Indian Congress Party and his son became a member of parliament. And so the dynasty rolled on.

I was one of the first overseas journalists to interview Benazir Bhutto in Islamabad when she became prime minister of Pakistan for the first time in 1988. I was her age and very much in awe of meeting Madam Prime-Minister-in-Waiting. It was nearly midnight when my turn came and this beautiful, charismatic thirty-year-old was curled up in an armchair. Halfway through our meeting – on the pretence that she felt in need of moral support – she elegantly uncurled and went off to find her husband, Asif Zardari, with whom she had entered an arranged marriage less than two years before.

The PM's consort had been catching up on some sleep and arrived claiming that, although his wife was about to become prime minister and his father was in the National Assembly, he wasn't a political animal at all. They joked informally together, and it transpired that Asif had already been persuaded by his wife to make one unusual sacrifice to help her political career. 'I've stopped him playing polo,' she admitted, 'because he kept having accidents and I think I've got enough worries already without him falling off ponies.' Their baby son, Bilawal, had only recently been born and I marvelled at all that this charismatic leader was taking on. Her father, Zulfikar Ali Bhutto, had been executed by General Zia's military regime the year my mother was elected prime minister. She had also lost two brothers.

Asif enlightened me that their arranged marriage had come about after his family first broached the subject of a wife with him. Asif replied, 'Get me Benazir and then I'll get married.' He added, 'She was the most eligible girl in the world and I presumed I was the most eligible guy in town.' They met in London where he wooed her with dozens of roses, a crate of mangoes from Fortnum and Mason, and boxes of *marrons glacés* – one of her favourite sweets.

I asked them if there wasn't a hint of unreality about their lives now that they seemed to be embodying Kennedy-style youth, promise and glamour. Benazir admitted that there was. 'It's like a fairytale or storybook. Sometimes I wonder how did it happen, how did I get here?'

Fifteen years later, on 27 December 2007, while staying in a hotel in Chiang Rai in northern Thailand, I turned on the television to hear the news that Benazir had been assassinated. I couldn't help but feel sad and admire the sheer courage of the children of political leaders who, despite having been on the inside looking out, still have the guts and commitment to follow in their parents' (or grandparents') footsteps. It was certainly not something I had ever aspired to.

Media coverage usually suggests that prime ministerial and presidential travels are made in red-carpeted luxury, with perfectly organised welcome ceremonies, guards of honour, photo calls and fulsome toasts to eternal friendship between the host and guest countries over lavish banquets. Not always, I can assure you. I remember watching my mother dutifully walking up and down rows of impeccably turned-out soldiers in ceremonial attire at some far-flung airport, when the person next to me enquired, 'Why is your mother inspecting the guard of honour to the tune of *The Godfather*?' I couldn't answer but I did have to giggle.

In 1983, the Commonwealth Heads of Government Meeting was held in India. The retreat for the Heads was at the Taj Holiday Villa in Goa. Visitors to this popular Indian resort will know that the tourist blurb proclaims in rhapsodical prose that Goa has 'fifty miles of beautiful beaches' and other facilities offering the perfect escape. Dad found it a more tense experience, particularly when, on the first night, the telephone in their chalet rang at some pre-dawn hour and a perky little voice said, with an element of satisfaction, 'Just testing.' The electricity was off more often than on, and when the lights failed for the umpteenth time Dad was moved to stride on to the balcony and declare in a stentorian voice, 'This place is very high on the buggeration factor.'

The buggeration factor for me nearly scuppered my chance to travel on *QE2*, something I had been looking forward to ever since my childhood holidays on the Isle of Wight when I first saw her sail into Southampton. It was spring 2008, the day Heathrow's new Terminal 5 opened. I was flying to Los Angeles to join the ship and I headed off, braced for tiresome teething problems and unexplained delays. No such thing – at first. I put my passport into the machine and it promptly spat out my boarding pass. I deposited my bags and before I knew it was in the British Airways lounge with time on my hands. As I boarded the flight to Los Angeles I congratulated the crew on how well all seemed to be functioning. Silly me.

We sat on the tarmac for a good couple of hours, the highlights of which were the occasional flight-deck announcement. 'Sorry about this, ladies and gentlemen, but this is the first day Terminal 5 has been operating and information is at a premium around here.' Well, I thought, if *they* can't find out what's going on, what hope for the rest of us? The crew sounded increasingly frustrated. Then, forty minutes later: 'The computer has our flight down as already left so they aren't loading any bags aboard.' I started to feel rather sorry for the lovely girl sitting across from me whose last day it was aged twenty-nine. She was off to Las Vegas to see her thirtieth birthday in, but neither she nor her party frock were yet on their way.

Eventually we did manage lift-off and both my bags arrived at Los Angeles airport without delay. Not everyone was so lucky. When I boarded QE2 with seventy other passengers, there were but a handful of bags between them. Their luggage did eventually arrive, ten days later, but even then there were setbacks. As we completed the lifeboat drill, sitting around in lifejackets between the slot machines in the casino, one lady told me that her bag was delivered to her hotel from a later flight, only to get lost again somewhere between hotel and ship. Needless to say, the sheer opulence of the vessel and the efficiency of the crew managed to soothe even the most annoyed of guests, and my public speaking seemed to be well received. Well, I do have rather a good track record with larger-than-life iron ladies.

My return to Los Angeles reminded me of a previous adventure in California, when I was staying in Palm Springs out in the desert. Dolores Hope, wife of the legendary entertainer Bob Hope (whom I had met at a White House dinner), kindly invited me to drop in to visit their spectacular home on my way to the airport. The building has become something of a local landmark with its bold design and imaginative, curvy shape which has been variously likened to Darth Vader's helmet or a flying saucer. For decades Bob and Dolores hosted fabulous parties for golfers and celebrities during the desert classic tournaments.

Dolores, who was in her eighties and quite a character, took me outside to point out some features of this desert oasis and which road I should take to the airport. We were standing on a glossy, well-watered, beautifully manicured piece of grass – in stark contrast to the parched, bleached, cactus-studded landscape all around us. The reason for this lush lawn soon became apparent. It was Bob's practice green at the end of a par-three fairway, and the automatic sprinkler system whooshed into action without warning. Dolores, surprisingly sprightly for her age, legged it back to the house through the wall of spray while I, in footwear less made for sprinting, got drenched. I drove all the way to the airport with my shoes squelching on the car pedals.

On a 1990s trip to Washington, DC, as a tourist, I decided to go on one of the public tours of the White House. I joined the line on a chilly, dark, wintry morning to be sure of getting one of that day's limited numbers of visitor tickets, and managed it.

The first time I had visited the White House was in 1979, when I'd accompanied my mother there during Jimmy Carter's presidency. It was shortly before Christmas and the decorations were magical. One of the staff told me that they start working on them around March.

The First Lady organised carol singing in the East Room for the after-dinner entertainment. In this historic white-panelled room, which had witnessed the lying-in-state of seven presidents, including Abraham Lincoln and John F. Kennedy, we were given hand-scripted carol sheets rolled up as scrolls and fastened with a gold presidential seal. I sat next to Mrs Carter in the front row. As the music started, she whispered to me that she had left her spectacles up in their private apartment and asked if I could tell her what was coming next. I spent the entire carol-singing session discreetly – I hope – prompting her: 'Away in a Manger' or 'The Twelve Days of Christmas'.

Later, in November 1988, I was 'daughter-of-the-British-PM guest' again when the entire family was invited to Ronald Reagan's dazzling farewell banquet. Reagan, a long-time friend of my mother's (my father always called theirs a 'mutual admiration society') was due to retire after a second term in office. Standing next to Barbara Bush, wife of President-Elect George, as we waited to go in, I engaged in some small talk. I liked Barbara; she was a jolly soul and good for a laugh. Exasperated with the delay, she complained, 'Politics consists of rushing, then waiting!' I couldn't agree more.

Eleven circular tables were decorated with thousands of pink roses arranged in giant balls like scoops of strawberry ice cream. The Marine bands, resplendent in red tunics, played as we all trooped in. The luscious menu on that occasion included Baby Lobster Bellevue, Caviar Yogurt Sauce and Roast Saddle of Veal. Fellow guests included such disparate characters as Dolores Hope, Mikhail Baryshnikov, Loretta Swit, George and Barbara Bush, the Reverend Billy Graham, David Hockney, Henry Kissinger, Colin Powell, Tom Selleck, Andrew Lloyd Webber, Sarah Brightman, Dick Cheney, Tom Wolfe and the actress Loretta Young. Dad and I had Nancy Reagan on our table, along with Dolores Hope, Billy Graham and Malcolm Forbes, publisher of *Forbes* magazine.

President Reagan expressed his sadness at this last meeting with my mother 'in this capacity'. They had always been deeply fond of each other, besides being so similar politically, and it was with some emotion that she told him he had 'restored faith in the American dream, the dream of boundless opportunity built in enterprise, individual effort and personal generosity'.

Now, a few years later, I was back at the White House as a 'civilian', in an orderly line along with scores of other folk, as our guide pointed out roped-off areas that I had once wandered through with presidents and generals.

The rooster one decade, the feather duster soon after!

Much of my latter travelling has been done as a working journalist, and has featured some rather unusual assignments. When Richard Branson and his UK 2000 Group were given the task of sprucing up Britain, starting with London's Trafalgar Square, they opted to follow the example of those who ran Disneyland. One senior executive of the London project had apparently been impressed by what she'd experienced in California. 'The ladies in the loos all had maps to direct you to the Haunted House and other attractions, and the ice-cream vendors knew exactly where the nearest loo was. Every member of staff made you feel so welcome.'

This gave the editor of one Sunday supplement the idea of despatching me to Disneyland to sample their much-vaunted indoctrination at the Disney University in Orlando, Florida. At this air-conditioned seat of learning, raw recruits are turned into model employees or 'cast members' who never miss a chance to slip in another 'Have a nice day' – delivered in the Mickey Mouseapproved tone. In a two-storey concrete building half a mile from the turrets of Cinderella's Castle, I took my place in a large classroom. Next to me was a guy who was there second time round, having got through college on his salary from working on Big Thunder, a Wild West roller. The emphasis was on work, even though students would mostly be dealing with excited holiday-makers. Beth, the teacher, enthused, 'There are days when you feel you can't smile at sixty thousand people, but the atmosphere snaps you out of it.'

What most fascinated me was the tour behind the scenes. Actually, it was mostly under the scenes, because the Magic Kingdom is serviced via a network of underground tunnels colour-coded so cast members surface in the right zone. I went out with the cleaning crew on the dawn shift and their effectiveness was impressive: the pavements were hosed down and left not so much clean as polished to a gleaming perfection. Wielding dustpans and brushes, this formidable team live on their reputation that they can scoop up a kid's dropped ice-cream cone almost before it hits the ground.

I was even given a chance to be Pluto for a few hours; a role I quickly came to understand was far harder than it looked, once I was all togged up in padding and acrylic fur on a sizzling August day. Inside these amazing costumes, temperatures can hit 140°F, and even the installation of NASA-type cooling systems can't prevent it from being anything but a thoroughly sweaty occupation.

For a photo call with other characters outside the castle, it was suggested that I slip out of my Pluto person and into a long dress and waist-length blonde wig to become Maid Marian. 'Good Luck!' I whispered to the ladies in the make-up and wardrobe departments who were put in charge of this colossal transformation. The photo call was quite a giggle. Robin Hood and I, Goofy, Mickey and Donald lined up for the photograph before Disneyland opened, the idea being that we'd finish before the first visitors came through the turnstiles. We ran late, and soon there was a long line of autograph hunters. I signed away, too, feeling rather chuffed. The first autographs were quite legible, a stylish 'Maid Marian', but as the novelty wore off they deteriorated to an 'MM' squiggle.

Then there were the assignments I was sent on which involved me getting in action-mode. Bob-sledding in Cervinia, an Italian ski resort on the other side of the Matterhorn from Zermatt, probably gave me the most petrifying thirty-three seconds of my life. I went down in a 'taxi' bob – at number three, with another passenger in second place, and a driver and brakeman completing the crew. 'Hang on tightly,' I was told. As if this instruction was necessary. One of the hairiest bends on the helter-skelter is called Curva Bianca, which may sound like an aperitif to be enjoyed overlooking Portofino on a summer's evening, but sadly, is nothing like that. The G-force as we negotiated it was vicious. When we juddered to a halt across the finish line, I felt as if I'd been in an industrial-sized tumble drier with the setting turned to high.

In 1988, I was lucky enough to be sent as a reporter to both the winter Olympics in Calgary, Canada, and the summer games in Seoul, South Korea. In Calgary, I was assigned to write a feature for the *Daily Mail* with the headline, 'Beach Bums with a Spirit of Adventure'. I had immense fun tracking down Olympic entrants from warm countries where winter sports were totally unknown, or where the only ice was in the drinks. Two of my favourites were John Reeve and John Foster, middle-aged men from the US Virgin Islands, whose enviable suntans came from long hours of tough training on the Caribbean beaches back home. Palm trees and bob-sleds don't normally go together, but there was a palm tree proudly emblazoned on the side of their bob as it flashed across the finishing line of the Olympic track. The Netherlands Antilles (postage-sized islands off the coast of Venezuela) had also produced a bob-sledding team, and Mexico was represented by four hilarious brothers on leave from their day jobs as waiters in a restaurant in Dallas, Texas.

Jamaica hadn't quite despatched half a steel band but Freddie Powell, one of the middle men in the four-man bob, is a reggae vocalist and his team has cut a record entitled 'Hobbin and a'Bobbin', which was progressing up the charts in Montego Bay to aid their fundraising efforts. There was even Riviera chic and a royal presence in the shape of Prince Albert of Monaco, whose brakeman, Gilbert Bessi, was enjoying a change from his croupier duties in the Monte Carlo casino. The newcomers created a thriving rent-a-bob market. One Canadian owner thoughtfully towed his bob through a Calgary carwash to ensure that it was hired to the Mexicans in a gleaming state.

There were other fascinating rarities in the Olympic Village, such as cross-country skiers from the Guatemalan rainforests of Central America, and even a lone Fijian. I warmed to these people's 'Don't worry, be happy' mentality. Their talk, once over the finish line, was not of the earnest, technical variety – how they could shave fractions of a second off their times – but about which of Calgary's nightspots they were planning to adjourn to for some exuberant après-bobbing.

For the British, the focus of the Calgary Olympics was a little-known ski jumper from Britain (our first and only). Born Michael Edwards in sedate Cheltenham, Gloucestershire, he became better known as 'Eddie the Eagle'. He was terrific value to the tabloid hacks – an amateur, a one-man comedy show who moved headline writers to hail him as 'Mr Magoo on Skis'. He was a plasterer who had only put on skis for the first time a couple of years earlier and who shot from anonymity to household-name stardom. I found his mother and interviewed her, asking when she had first sensed his Olympic spirit. 'Oh, I knew from when he was a toddler,' she told me confidently. 'He used to bounce up and down on the family sofa before jumping off in the direction of the coal bucket.'

Having established myself as a 'go anywhere' travel hack and written my first book, *Lloyd on Lloyd*, about the marriage between popular tennis stars Chris Evert and John Lloyd, I was invited to appear on and contribute to television and radio shows.

Perhaps my favourite was BBC Radio Four's *Loose Ends*. Hosted by dear Ned Sherrin, it was an immensely successful programme which had been broadcasting to the nation from the bowels of Broadcasting House on Saturday mornings since 1986. In his autobiography, Ned said the premise of the series was 'to surround an "old fart" (me) with bright, pushy younger interviewers and correspondents who would keep me on my toes'. They included Stephen Fry, Jonathan Ross, Emma Freud, Bob Elms Craig Charles, Victoria Mather and many more – and me.

The *Radio Times* set up a cover story on Ned and his team. The photograph was to be in a classroom setting, with a St Trinian's slant. Alas, on the day of the shoot, I was overseas, so the decision was made to put a framed portrait of me on the classroom wall as a tennis captain. Not that my playing was up to much, but I was an avid Wimbledon fan and my authorly claim to fame at that time included the biography of the Lloyds, which had been number one on the bestseller list for five consecutive weeks.

Returning from my trip, I didn't expect to see much of this tennis-captain-fame on the cover and I wasn't disappointed. When it was printed, the downward stroke of the 'R' of *Radio Times* sliced vertically through my photo. The story of how I was nearly on the cover became a running gag.

The programme became so successful that writers Victor Lewis-Smith and Paul Sparks edited a book about it, catching the flavour of the show meticulously. I was asked to contribute a chapter on the topic of being a *Loose Ends* reporter. I wrote about the producer's brainwave for my first assignment, 'Thatcher off to the Tip.' It was to be a tough, investigative six-minute item on garbology (the science of trash, garbage, rubbish, call it what you will). The idea came from a minor sensation in the national press concerning some kids who'd found a finger on a tip near Bristol. One pathologist claimed it was a human finger, but a second opinion downgraded it to a rubber one. Wielding a microphone, I sought out the licensed totters in charge of fingers and other 'finds'. One told me he had the filthiest job in the world. I asked him what the incentive was. 'Hopefully, we'll find something one day and be able to retire.' Not fingers, presumably.

Following hard on the heels of that inaugural contribution, I was given a variety of other off-beat little assignments including *Loose Ends'* first underwater interview, a piece about shoplifting, learning to hot-air balloon with the man who taught Richard Branson, and a guest appearance as a cheerleader with a professional American football team, the LA Rams. The underwater number, entitled 'Deep Sea Jiving', required me to present myself at a posh Knightsbridge health club and submerge myself (in swimsuit) in the pool for an underwater serenade on the saxophone by musician Peter Thomas. Apart from nearly drowning, it was a novel experience. I asked Peter if anything else sounded like a saxophone underwater or if it was a uniquely refined, pure musical experience? According to Peter, whales sound fairly similar. Sadly, my in-depth questions in the shallow end made little headway through the chlorinated gallons of water, so we had to surface (my sole effort at being upwardly mobile).

My mother's fans were in the habit of proclaiming that Maggie had put the 'Great' back in 'Great Britain', and she had a universally acknowledged reputation for having a black belt in the art of lecturing voters and giving television interviews without bothering to pause. On another *Loose Ends* assignment, to the Budgie Beano in Birmingham, I soon discovered that talkative owners have talkative birds. Thank goodness my mother never owned a parrot. Some birds, alas, were overcome with stage fright and wouldn't utter a word, but I was impressed by one with a flair for languages, which squawked away in Japanese. I will never make it as a budgie judge, though. 'Is this Miss World?' I asked admiring a rather fetching specimen.

'No. It's *Mr* Universe,' corrected a bird buff.

My next 'sound' assignment was in the gents in the basement of Broadcasting House. The producer had noticed a news item that a West Country male choir was offering to audition aspiring choristers in the privacy of their own bathrooms, so Barry Rose, who was the Master of Choirs at King's School, Canterbury, rendezvoused with me in the loos to assess the acoustics. Don't laugh. Bathrooms and Tube stations really are the best places if you want your voice to sound like you've always dreamed. I was rather pleased with this item, as it didn't waste any time deflating the puffed-up egos of purring presenters. 'Carol Thatcher going down the plughole with a load of bathroom baritones' was Ned's line to finish my piece back in the studio.

When the LA Rams came to Wembley to pit their skills against fellow American footballers Denver Broncos, they brought their very own cheerleading squad, and I went along to find out what was involved in becoming a high-kicking, ring-of-confidence-smiling, tanned, toned, dancing, chanting Barbie doll. My pom-pom routine was a messy disaster (absolutely no co-ordination or style), but I had high hopes that my Cheshire Cat grin might pass muster. Not a chance. 'It's too stressed out,' the champ cheerleader in charge informed me.

'Too what?'

Before each show, Ned and his team had a read-through for timing and potential libels (plenty of scope for those). We sat round a table and, once the sound checks had been done, I braced myself for any mention of my ma and the politics of her government. Special attention was paid to the morning's newspapers and the ten o'clock news, which Ned always insisted on hush for, in case it announced the death of anyone who was in the *Loose Ends* firing line.

One Saturday morning in 1986, we were all going through the newspapers as usual when someone spotted a headline in the *Daily Mail*: 'Engaged! It's Official – Mark and Diane to Marry.' It added, 'After dancing until the early hours, Maggie's son breaks the good news.' My brother had announced his forthcoming marriage to his beautiful, blonde Texan girlfriend, Diane Burgdorf, in the columns of *The Times* and *Telegraph* and the *Mail* had picked it up.

The producer could hardly believe his luck when he discovered that there was a Bride and Home exhibition on at Alexandra Palace. His idea? To send the spinster sister of the bridegroom to report on it, so off I went. The first person I met was a herbal guru who introduced me to 'love bags' of herbs and essential oils which apparently induced warmth of spirit and pleasing thoughts. Just the thing for newlyweds, although the guru had some pragmatic advice: 'I strongly recommend that you never have the sleep mix and the love mix in the same room because it can lead to certain problems.'

On the morning of the wedding, Valentine's Day, 1987, Ned opened the show with the sound of wedding bells and gleefully proclaimed that the show would be live from the Savoy Chapel (the venue for my brother's wedding), which it thankfully wasn't. I made my contribution and was allowed to escape with my hat early to head for the Strand in the hope of turning up before the bride.

After the disorderly conduct of the *Loose Ends* studio, the calming sound of hymns and the scent of roses wafted over me in the chapel, and even I felt romantic. At thirty-three, and having not had much success in the love stakes, I'd decided I was never going to marry, but it was pure pleasure to see my parents' pride at their son's wedding. I was sitting next to Dad, and after Mark and Diane had completed their vows he whispered: 'That's done it!'

There was a splendid lunch and party afterwards. So many Texan friends and relatives of the bride had flown over that I became an instant expert on the Lone Star State. Someone raved so much about cowboy boots that when, years later, I passed a factory outlet for them in Florida, I hopped out and bought several pairs. One guest gave me a slightly over-long and rather far-fetched spiel about castrating cattle down on the ranch, until a pal of his interrupted. 'If bullshit was snow, you could ski in Texas,' he told me.

'Handbagging' as a term denoting Maggie-on-the-warpath slipped into common parlance as a potent political verb during my mother's term in Number Ten. She had banged her hands and her bag on the table during a European summit and demanded that Britain be given a rebate on its contributions. She got her way, and that rebate is now worth around £2 billion a year. I guess because of Mum's association with handbags ever since, I received a call one day from someone on the fashion desk of *The Times* asking me if I – as official 'Daughter of Handbagging' – would like to review a posh new handbag with a hefty price tag, which was apparently greatly in demand by the capital's fashionistas.

'Yes, please' was my reply, even though I freely admit that 'scruffy' always has, and always will, do for me. What a hoot, though. I had to give it a go.

As Mum had enjoyed such knockout successes with her handbag, I like to think that I can assess the credibility of any such accessory. Maggie's handbags exuded menace towards striking trade unionists, Argentine dictators and Eurocrats, and doubled as mobile filing cabinets for a confetti of political paperwork, cans of 'firm hold' hairspray and tins of throat pastilles to revive vocal chords which had made one speech too many. One of my favourite photographs is of my mother looking down and concentrating on a statement – or something of that nature. On the table is the handbag. The photographer snapped the scene with her slightly out of focus and so she co-stars with the bag. The bag appears to sense it is centre-stage: the handles don't flop but stay upright as if the accessory was in high-alert mode and might be pressed into action to 'handbag' a target.

The pinnacle of Mum's handbagging fame surely came when one of her black Ferragano clutch bags with a snap gold buckle and letter of authentication signed by her appeared as a lot in a charity auction to raise funds for breast cancer. The diminutive bag attracted a final bid of £100,000 (Cherie Booth's managed a mere £350).

Inspired, perhaps, by my mother, I began my own collection of handbags, most of which were outrageous and rarely gained maternal approval. Some are in tones best described as a clash between the colours found in a box of chocolate Smarties and those favoured by the graffiti artist Banksey. A conversation with my mother might go something like this:

'Where did you get *that* bag, Carol?'

'Oh, I spotted it when window shopping.'

'That, dear, is why I never walk.'

My favourite is a wooden-sided model which looks like the bottom of a cello. I found it in a tiny boutique in Tokyo, but delayed the purchase until the following day. When I returned, it wasn't on the shelf. My disappointment evaporated when the shop assistant dived under the counter and emerged waving it. 'I knew you'd come back,' she declared triumphantly.

Girlfriends with far better taste than mine occasionally groan at some of my most garish purchases. 'Oh, Carol, no!' they cry.

My response is usually the same. 'Well, my mum invented the verb "handbagging",' I say. 'What's your excuse?'

I was childishly excited about the prospect of reviewing the glamorous 'Manhattan Croc' – although I had to admit I had never spotted any crocodiles cruising the sidewalks of Fifth Avenue. When it arrived by courier, I wondered if I had been sent a High Street imitation by mistake. It was certainly a stratosphere away from the Maggie-style handbags of yesteryear. Surely even the sparkliest diamanté and shiniest red plastic could not justify the £5,200 price tag? Yes, you read correctly. Somewhere beyond the M25, that kind of money still serves as a deposit on a first-time buyer's home.

On closer inspection of the said handbag, I realised that, in my haste, I had misjudged the situation. This wasn't made of plastic and diamanté, it was plastic- and diamanté-*effect*, wrought from real crocodile skin and studded with a hundred and twenty-four genuine diamonds, and it was from a London-based Japanese designer called Shizue Nobuta, renowned for creating beautiful bags 'the likes of which you'll never have seen before'.

Kylie Minogue owned two Manhattan Crocs, I was informed.

Everyone else was saving up to buy . . . one. I had my doubts, but already the bag was growing on me. Capacious it wasn't, if you're the sort of person who carries around a make-up war chest, but once I had edited out my sunglasses case and my Filofax, I just about managed. I guess the owner of a Manhattan Croc leads a champagne existence with their minder trotting two steps behind looking after their surplus paraphernalia.

I invited the bag on a short tour of London to assess whether it had the potential to change my life. We began with a trip on the Underground (I'm sure the bag scowled) and managed not to get mugged. We raced along to a performance of *The Lion King* – as the bag had once been a croc, I thought perhaps it would enjoy a jungle musical. A woman a few rows in front, seemingly under the misapprehension that I had scalped a jaw-snapping croc for my trendy new accessory, shot me a disapproving look. The bag glistered back.

But it was only during the interval that the bag and I finally bonded. Thanks to the glinting diamonds, I was able to retrieve it from the darkness under my seat (seconds ahead of fellow theatre-goers) and sprint to the bar to be first in the queue for a glass of vino. By now I had started to admire the highly buffed, glossy ruby skin. Was it designed with Sven-Göran Eriksson's flamboyant Italian partner, Nancy Dell'Olio in mind? It would undoubtedly have matched her scarlet outfit and high-rise stilettos and doubled as a weapon of mass destruction. But did it suit me?

It certainly attracted attention. There was an embarrassing

scene at Tate Modern when I took the Croc to see the Indian-born British sculptor Anish Kapoor's vast new sculpture and the bag eclipsed the exhibit. The Croc's natural home, I discovered, is not stashed under a seat in a darkened theatre but on display, preferably in a fashionable art gallery. It would have turned up its nose at the mock-croc square on which my mother founded her handbagging reputation. This croc was interested in premieres, not political conferences. In short, the Manhattan Croc is for girls whose lives come gift-wrapped rather than those who are stalled in proletarian packaged gear. It is overloaded with feel-good factor – but only for the truly loaded.

When I related all this to Crawfie, who as Keeper of Maggie's Handbags for decades had a far superior knowledge of my mother's personal accessories, she told me a tale which showed that, even under the most urgent and dreadful circumstances, Mum and her handbag were inseparable. The occasion was the Brighton bombing at the Tory party conference. Immediately after the bomb had gone off and Mum and Dad had checked on each other and their immediate staff, a fireman arrived in the prime ministerial suite to warn them there was a danger that the ceiling might cave in and that they must evacuate immediately.

Crawfie quickly set about gathering up some of Mum's clothes and personal possessions. Mum and Dad remained calm but the fear of a further bomb caused a certain frisson in the room. Then came the question of what to do with the leader's precious copy of the keynote speech she was due to deliver the following morning.

Crawfie came up with the perfect solution: 'We'll pop it into her handbag. She'll never be parted from that.' And I'm just as inseparable from some of my old favourites.

Chapter Eleven

FISH OUT OF WATER

OVER THE YEARS friends, colleagues and acquaintances have told me that they remember exactly where they were and what they were doing when news broke that my mother had resigned as prime minister, voted out by the party she'd led to three successive general election victories. I certainly remember this most dramatic episode in British political history all too well.

A year previously, two years after Mum was returned to power for a third term, on the slogan 'Moving Forward with Maggie', Dad had unsuccessfully tried to persuade her to retire on a high in the tenth-anniversary year of her becoming prime minister. She had declined, feeling she still had much to do. A few days after the historic polling day that gave her that third term, Dad and I were both in the flat at Number Ten and he was fixing us a drink. 'In a year,' he told me, 'she'll be so unpopular you won't believe it.' Prophetic words.

The first signs of trouble came with a leadership challenge from Sir Anthony Meyer, followed by the furore over the poll tax and European intervention. Dad was right, although the chain of events that eventually led to her downfall took a little longer than he predicted.

As far as my father was concerned, the last couple of weeks of November 1990 began ordinarily enough. In his desk diary, he wrote:

Monday 19th: *PM ONLY away to Paris.* Then, in the margin, *DT's Ford estate, MOT due on 30th.*

Monday 26th: *DT refused dinner for PM of Spain.*

In the intervening days, my parents had sat down and signed a thousand Number Ten Christmas cards – giving themselves writer's cramp. There were always two cards, the prime minister's and another one which the staff could send. They were always a bit of a production. One year, in which Chequers looked quite magical in the snow, Mum got the photographer down to take the shot for the following year, before the white stuff turned to slush.

At the beginning of November, Sir Geoffrey Howe, once a close friend and ally of my mother's, had resigned as deputy prime minister over his disagreement with Mum's European policy and suggested, in his resignation speech a fortnight later, that others do the same. In the light of Howe's speech, Michael Heseltine, disgruntled former cabinet minister turned backbench MP, challenged my mother for leadership and forced a ballot. The news was both shocking and extremely worrying. Mum was due to fly to Paris that week for a meeting of the Conference on Security and Cooperation in Europe (CSCE), and decided to go ahead regardless of the ballot. Many of my journalist contacts had warned me that she was in danger of losing the vote.

At Chequers, I found her in her dressing room the morning she was leaving, going through her red boxes. Surrounded by files as usual, she told me, 'I might lose, but I don't think I will.'

I wished her luck, collected my weekend bag, and headed for the door and my drive back to London. One of the staff came out to see me off. In utterly neutral tones, she said, 'Goodbye, Miss Thatcher. I hope we see you again soon.' It was if she was tactfully distancing herself, ready for the next occupant. As I drove out of the inner gates onto the long drive, I took a lingering look at Chequers in my rear-view mirror. Almost without thinking, I said to myself, 'I'll never come here again.' The loss felt tangible.

Despite my worries and Dad's pessimism, Mum won the first round. When I got home that evening, there were lots of calls on my answering machine from friends and journalists saying, 'She can still win. She should fight on.' Dad felt differently and was canvassing political friends and allies to persuade her not to stand for the second ballot.

When my mother saw her cabinet colleagues one by one the following day, they told her – almost to a man – that, while they would support her if she stood, she should resign to avoid 'humiliation' and let someone who could definitely win it stand against Heseltine. All afternoon, my telephone rang and I was pleased to have an excuse to get out of the house. The *Evening Standard* had asked me to judge their Pub of the Year competition and then I'd arranged to have dinner with Dad and Alistair McAlpine at a club in Mayfair. My mother was staying home and working on her speech for the Commons the following day. As I closed my front door, I thought, 'Thank God I don't have to worry about her for the next few hours.'

One of the pubs on the list was virtually my local, the White Horse on Parson's Green. Two of my fellow judges were Angus McGill and Willie Rushton, and they poured me a large glass of wine and cheered me up by announcing gleefully that they were considering standing for the second ballot. By the time I got to dinner, I was well-wined. Alistair McAlpine ordered champagne, with the instruction, 'Everyone knows who we are, so we all have to look frightfully up.' I slurped my champagne and looked across at Dad. I could tell he was struggling to be jolly.

Privately, Alistair told me that the cabinet had defected one by one, and that Mum had decided to resign. I couldn't believe it. 'But yesterday, in Paris, she said she would fight to win. It's not like her – she doesn't back down,' I said. The shock of the news took time to sink in. Mum was Britain's first female prime minister and, after eleven-and-a-half years, one of the longest serving. Now the end loomed for her.

I accompanied Dad home, asking our driver to drop us at Horse Guards Parade to avoid the TV cameras and photographers we knew would be massed outside Downing Street. It was dark and windy and Dad was wrapped in his favourite cape. Arm in arm, we trudged across the wet gravel, looking at the eerie glow of television lights outside Number Ten. Halfway across the parade ground, Dad stopped and turned to look at me. He pushed up his glasses and I could see tears in his eyes.

'Oh, it's just the disloyalty of it all,' he whispered, and we hugged. It was the only time I ever saw him cry.

'Look, Dad,' I said, fighting back my own tears, 'what really matters now is Mum. It's going to be a hell of a shock and we have to support her. We have to do everything we can to make it easier.' We walked despondently to the police box at the back of Number Ten. The officer came out and I asked him, 'Please see my father up the steps?'

As Dad turned to go, I told him, 'Goodnight. Let's all be strong and see what tomorrow brings.' I doubted my own words, and none of us slept well that night – in my case, not least because I took several late-night calls from friends of my mother's who were trying to console me.

It was just after eight o'clock the following morning when my father rang, his voice sounding strained. 'There have been all sorts of consultations and your mother—' he began.

'I know, Dad,' I interrupted, sparing him the ordeal of actually saying the words. There was silence, and we finally said goodbye. There was nothing more to say.

I called her secretary, Joy Robilliard, at Number Ten to be told that my mother was not taking any calls. 'She's OK, but a bit weepy and liable to break down if anyone says anything nice to her.' Joy's voice, too, sounded strange.

'I'm not going to speak to her because I think I might cry,' I said.

'She's not seeing anyone until she makes her speech.'

Desperate not to be cornered by the media, I decided to keep a low profile at my house in Fulham. I let the answering machine pick up the endless stream of calls. I had already invited people over for dinner that evening, an event planned weeks in advance, and I decided not to cancel. After all, the show must go on. I nipped down to the supermarket immediately after Dad called, to buy some extra alcohol. I thought we might need it.

I returned home to hear the telephone ringing, and I answered with a fluttering heart. It was a journalist from the *Evening Standard* who informed me, 'There is a strong rumour your mother is going to resign.'

'Thank you,' I interjected. 'I shall turn on the telly.' And I did.

It was 9.25 a.m. when the announcement came. It was brief and explosive, a short statement signalling the end of Mum's tenure as prime minister. 'Having consulted widely among my colleagues,' she said, using words I know she would almost certainly have penned herself, 'I have concluded that the unity of the party and the prospects of victory in a general election would be better served if I stood down to enable cabinet colleagues to enter the ballot for the leadership. I should like to thank all those in cabinet and outside who have given me such dedicated support.'

All day the telephone rang and flowers arrived at the door. Friends from around the world were asking, 'How could this happen?' However furious I was, I told myself that it wasn't for me to say anything to the journalists waiting outside my house. But I was deeply distressed at the way my mother had been treated, and, of course, I worried about the devastating impact such rejection would have on a woman whose entire adult life had been devoted to politics. She knew no other.

Neil Kinnock, the leader of the opposition, had proposed a motion of no confidence in the government, in the light of the leadership contest. Mum was due to respond in the Commons that afternoon. I wondered how she could face it. The no-confidence motion was almost a repeat of what had happened at the end of Jim Callaghan's government, when my mother had first seized the initiative. I could hardly bear to watch the televised debate: the thought of Mum breaking down and not being able to get through it was dreadful. When she rose to address the House at 4.50 p.m., I kept turning the telly on and off until I was sure she was OK. Needless to say, she rose to the challenge brilliantly, thundering for almost an hour to a packed House about Europe, Britain's high standing in the world, and the numerous achievements of her government. She spoke of the end of the Cold War, the success in the Falklands, the collapse of communism in Eastern Europe, and Britain's contribution to making the world a safer place.

Fighting a tickly cough and on her feet for almost an hour, she proclaimed, 'Eleven years ago we rescued this country from the perilous state the socialists had let it get to.' She added that the Conservatives had no intention of letting Labour 'run – or is it ruin? – this country', and affirmed, 'This House and this country can have confidence in this government today.' I was amazed. How on earth did she manage to pull that off?

When she had finished, one MP shouted, 'That's the spirit!' Another cried, 'You could wipe the floor with the lot of them!' When a Labour MP suggested she become governor of the Bank of England when she stepped down, there was much laughter and uproar. My mother, in a fetching royal-blue suit, jumped up, laughing, too. 'That's a very good idea. I hadn't thought of that!' she said, adding with a smile, 'Now, where were we? I'm enjoying this!' It was a stellar performance.

My father watched it at Number Ten with a friend and several drinks. He was bursting with pride when Mum returned, leaping up, moist-eyed, and telling her, 'That was wonderful . . . brilliant . . . magnificent!'

I rang Number Ten and, this time, was put straight through. 'I think you're a heroine,' I told her, when she picked up the phone. And then I burst into tears. 'I don't know how you made that speech,' I sobbed. 'It's just so awful what they've done – your party are complete shits.'

She sounded extremely calm. 'Well, they've done what the Labour Party didn't manage to do in three elections – defeat me,' she replied. Unable to hide her bitterness, she told me that at the end of her speech she had seen Conservatives she knew had voted against her cheering and waving their order papers. She rang off, telling me, 'I think my place in history is assured.'

That evening, my friends came to dinner as planned. After an emotional debate about the day's momentous events, we rounded the night off with a few large whiskies. The following morning there was a handful of journalists still standing outside my front gate. I couldn't help but recall my father's advice: 'Whales only get killed when they spout.' I called a friend to ask for some advice. 'Should I go and say anything or not?' He suggested it might be friendly to take the assembled press some coffee and at least say, 'Good morning.' I pointed out that such was my hangover that it would take me a good half-hour before I could confidently handle a tray of drinks, much less a civilised greeting.

The *Daily Mail* headline that morning summed up my feelings: 'She's Too Damn Good for Them.' The accompanying article said, 'Betrayed and rejected by her party, Margaret Thatcher gave up her power yesterday. She did so with a magnificent class that she alone of British politicians can produce. She announced her resignation as prime minister and then, undaunted, went to the Commons and defended her record with the speech of a lifetime.' Reading the other tributes, I almost felt as if Mum had won rather than lost.

In the final days at Downing Street, there was pandemonium. Mum had thrown her support behind John Major, whom – in the previous three years – she had appointed successively chief secretary to the Treasury, foreign secretary and chancellor of the exchequer. She was busy rallying support for him in her determination that Heseltine should not succeed. Meanwhile, Crawfie, Joy and others were scrambling around the flat, deciding what was staying, what was going into storage, and what was moving to my parents' new home in Dulwich, south London. 'I'll come and move my junk out,' I told them, only to find myself enlisted in a full-scale operation.

It was incredible how much stuff my parents had managed to accumulate in what was basically a rented furnished flat. The floor was covered with books, clothes, lamps, porcelain and half-filled dustbin liners. Dad and I in our respective cars ferried stuff up and down to Dulwich. Mark flew in from his new home in Dallas to help. The press were still camped outside doing their 'pieces to camera' about how history was being made inside, while – behind the curtains – my mother was padding about in her stockinged feet deciding whether one layer of paper or two would be sufficient to protect her favourite knick-knacks.

I had been working for several years as a pundit for TV-am and one of my hacking jobs had been to review the newspapers on the BBC's *Frost on Sunday* television programme. David Frost called me and asked if I would do a live report from outside Number Ten. Standing in front of the black-painted door that I had, for the past eleven years, considered the entrance to my parents' home, I pointed out that my mother – who was inside packing – was now wearing 'two hats'. I added, 'She is, of course, prime minister so she has all those responsibilities still, but she is preparing for re-emerging into the real world. For instance, an aide rushed into the sitting room yesterday and said, "Drop that packing case, Prime Minister. The White House is on the telephone" [about the crisis in Kuwait]. During the live broadcast, I was asked if my mother would be writing her memoirs. 'Right now,' I said, 'she could pen a very good handbook on how to do a fast move.'

As a result of my radio and TV comments, I found myself the recipient of a large mail bag, much of which offered unwavering support. My mother, of course, received thousands of letters of support – so many, in fact, that she had to put a notice in *The Times* thanking people and apologising for not being able to answer them all personally. But to this day I am surprised and grateful for those I received from members of the public who felt I needed cheering up, too. I took special comfort from long-standing friends who remained loyal throughout my mother's career, and long after it had ended. One told me, *'You said it all, baby. Sod the lot of 'em.'* Many letters were from strangers, who just needed an outlet. One wrote:

I feel that the Great has left Great Britain with your mother's departure – her brilliant speech in the House was a tour de force – one realised that no one could match her. What a lady. I watched ALL the Conservatives at the conclusion of her speech rise with acclaim and I hope they were ashamed. The rest of the world must think we are barmy, losing a leader whom they would give their eye teeth to have. We trusted her and she was so steadfast in what she thought was right for this country.

That correspondent was right. I am very proud of all my mother achieved, her honesty, integrity and directness. Not to mention her lack of the need for spin. I was especially proud of her dignity in the days and weeks that followed her public ousting from office. It was something others admired, too:

Dear Miss Thatcher,
May I take this opportunity to be another voice amongst countless who have written to you – to express my heartfelt admiration and respect for the way in which the Thatcher family endured these past weeks of tremendous pressure and strain. The extreme dignity which the Prime Minister displayed upon leaving Downing Street, and indeed throughout the ghastly ordeal, is something never to be forgotten. Her impeccable manner in the face of such adversity showed a kind of courage and strength one never

expects to see again. Your family has towered in noble, dignified strength throughout this tragedy, especially your mother, of whom you must be intensely proud.

Change is always hard, but particularly when your home for the last decade has been one of the most famous addresses in the world. The truth is that nothing prepares you for relinquishing membership of one of the world's most exclusive clubs. It wasn't just that my mother and father no longer lived at Ten Downing Street. Chequers – that splendid weekend retreat, where staff even leave the *Radio Times* open at the correct day – had been lost to them, too. However much you tell yourself that such properties only go with the job, when you are there they're yours. I knew that my parents would miss Chequers dreadfully, and felt my own sadness at never again enjoying that beautiful house.

Preparing to spend their final weekend there, my mother asked me, 'Do you want to come to Chequers, darling? It will be the last time.'

'No. I said goodbye to Chequers last weekend.' Knowing how they felt about the place, I wanted them to have their privacy.

Their final lunch there was with two friends at the small window table where they'd had their first meal. It was miserable. No one knew what to say. My mother, staring out of the window at the rose garden, broke a long silence. 'Look,' she said. 'There's a late rose.'

One of the guests later told me, movingly, 'Denis and Margaret were walking hand-in-hand in tears along the gallery that overlooked the Great Hall.'

In the last days at Number Ten, Mum followed minutely every aspect of the leadership ballot, and was thrilled when John Major won with a hundred and eighty-five votes against Heseltine's hundred and thirty-one. Her work was done. Now simply the Right Honourable Margaret Thatcher, MP for Finchley and Friern Barnet, she prepared to leave.

The staff lined up along the corridor and into the entrance hall, many weeping openly. When they broke into spontaneous applause, Mum could no longer hold back her own tears. Wiping her eyes, she had Crawfie check for any smudged mascara before she went outside into the glare of the television lights. Having made a short speech, she stepped into her waiting car, looking quite bewildered. As the camera flashguns lit up the dim interior, it was obvious that she was crying. Those photographs were bounced around the world, to become the most poignant images of her final days. The car swept away and headed south across the Thames to Dulwich. My parents said very little.

When the car arrived at its destination, there were more photographers and reporters waiting. As Mum emerged from the car one shouted, 'What are you going to do now?'

Her handbag hooked over her arm, my mother turned and gave a quick reply before striding purposefully into her new home. 'Work,' she said. 'That's all we have ever known.'

The first Sunday after my mother had left Number Ten,

I drove not to Chequers as usual but to the unfamiliar destination of Dulwich. The house wasn't their first choice – they had originally found a property they liked near Regent's Park but it needed too much work and neither Mum nor Dad had the time or the inclination to supervise. Invited to spend a weekend with a friend in Dulwich soon afterwards, they were told of an 'upmarket new estate' nearby and went to have a look. Wandering into a show house, they spotted a workman plastering a ceiling. Mum said, 'Gosh that looks interesting. How do you do that?' The chap looked down, saw who it was and almost fell off his ladder. Loving an instant solution, my mother took one look around the small estate of four or five houses in a cul-de-sac, pointed at the one that wasn't quite finished yet and said, 'We'll take that one.'

In the (now completed) sitting room, I found her reading the Sunday newspapers with the aid of a magnifying glass. This may not seem unusual, but in the previous eleven years she had rarely lifted a Sunday paper from the neatly laid-out selection on the sideboard at Chequers. 'I must keep in touch, keep up with the news. I must stay informed,' she explained, desperate to remain in the loop.

More than once I saw her, while watching some crisis on TV, instinctively reach for the phone before the thunderbolt realisation that it was now someone else's problem. She was at least able to retain her driver and police protection having left office, and the former told me that he began to avoid using Whitehall because, as their car passed Downing Street, she would look up wondering why they hadn't turned in. Then she would remember.

When Ronald Reagan visited London just after leaving office after two terms as president he tried to open the door of his car every time it stopped because for eight years he hadn't been in a vehicle which had halted before he had arrived.

Mum having left office a month before Christmas, my parents had to un-invite all the people who were due to come to Chequers, and arrange an alternative venue at the Dorchester. After years of pirouetting around in a long dress at seven o'clock most nights, ready to dash off and attend a dinner or make a speech, Mum found herself largely idle in the evenings. Now it was my father who, clad in dinner jacket, would prepare to go out while my mother looked on and enquired, 'What time will you be home, dear?' More often that not, she stayed in and cooked herself a poached egg on toast.

One night, TV-am's boss, Bruce Gyngell, invited her to a dinner party attended by David Frost and his wife, and Rupert Murdoch. Mum held up well, until she had to leave for a vote in the House at ten o'clock. After she'd gone, I asked Rupert Murdoch, who had spent a long time chatting to her, 'How do you think she is?'

'Absolutely shell-shocked,' he replied, 'but if I'd lost everything, so would I be.'

Dad, who had deliberately kept out of the limelight and previously done nothing to overshadow his famous wife, started coming into his own. When Mum became PM, security personnel told him he would have to sell his beloved Rolls-Royce with its personalised number plate, DT3, because it was so conspicuous to terrorists or kidnappers. He was heartbroken and initially asked if it would be enough to get rid of the personalised number plate, but they said no. Insisting that once a man has driven a Rolls he can never truly be happy without one, he sold his with great reluctance and announced he would buy a Ford. Mum thought this an overreaction, but Dad bought a blue Cortina station wagon and drove it into the ground over the next eleven years. It was a great car and he claimed to have never once opened the bonnet. Now that he was free of the shackles of office, he treated himself to another Rolls-Royce, in which he travelled to golf clubs up and down the country, as well as the odd board meeting.

My father's friends remained as loyal as ever, but many of my mother's friendships stopped with politics. She would be the first to say that when you're at the top you have lots of friends but as soon as you go, they gravitate – like bees to the new honey pot – to the next occupant of Number Ten. It's not just the loss of friends and power that hits home. It's the loss of privilege. She was still an MP, still passionate about politics, and still had to attend the House or her new London office most days, where she continued to put as much time and effort into her speeches and her constituency as ever. But she soon discovered the pain of commuting into central London. Without the traffic-jam-hopping benefits of the prime minister's car, complete with police outriders, the journey to Trafalgar Square took far longer than the previous seventeen minutes.

My parents also had to rediscover an everyday item they never used – keys. Not for a decade had there been the slightest possibility of being locked out or losing the front door keys, because there are no keys to Number Ten: the door opens on cue; and it's the same at Chequers. As for unlocking and starting your own car with those new-fangled keys, well that was a whole new world.

When my mother left Number Ten she had no idea how to make a phone call. She hadn't a clue about numbers, regional codes or dialling tones, for the simple reason that for more than a decade she hadn't lifted the receiver unless it was to hear a switchboard operator saying: 'Yes, Prime Minister, can I help you?' or 'Prime Minister, I have the president for you . . .' On one visit to their new home in Dulwich, I found the sitting room littered with phone numbers scrawled on Post-It notes. I asked why she never called me. 'Because I haven't got your number, dear,' she replied. Until then she'd simply asked the operator, 'Please get me Carol.'

I was worried she wouldn't be able to cope with ordinary tasks such as supermarket shopping. I couldn't imagine her wheeling a trolley up and down the aisles of her local Sainsbury's. Gingerly, I enquired if she would be able to manage the weekly shop. 'Good heavens, yes, dear!' she replied. 'I've opened enough of them.' Somehow, it just wasn't the same.

My mother was no longer prime minster and I would never again be introduced as 'the prime minister's daughter'. The shutters came down. After being in the goldfish bowl for so many years, I was suddenly back on the outside, looking in. It took years to acclimatise, although there were several moments that reminded me how passée I was. Sent on the famous Paris–Moscow–Beijing rally as a reporter, I found myself in the desert region between the Caspian and Aral seas in the former Soviet Union. The place was arid, dusty and barren to all compass points.

Reaching a check-point I commented to one of the drivers that it reminded me of the area in which my brother got lost during the Paris–Dakar rally.

Another driver chipped in that if the event needed more publicity I could easily be abandoned somewhere inhospitable.

'No,' someone volunteered realistically, 'that wouldn't achieve anything. Her mother's no longer prime minister.'

Who would look for me, let alone make a fuss?

Occasions like that gave me a taste of what it must be like to have been a waxwork in Madame Tussaud's when someone decides your recognition factor is no longer high enough and you are shipped off to the vaults.

My mother remained busy and coped best with the transition by embarking on a series of overseas visits. She took the post of chancellor of the College of William and Mary in Virginia, one of America's oldest universities, founded by royal charter in the seventeenth century. She still marked some anniversaries with the

Reagans and travelled widely, checking into a hotel's sumptuous presidential suite even though she no longer held presidential status. She also stayed in touch with Augusto Pinochet, the former Chilean leader who had been such an ally during the Falklands war.

Dad, Mum and I went together to Moscow in 1993. A lunch party for the Gorbachevs was held at the British embassy, a grand and elegant building with views across the river to the Kremlin and the gold and onion domes of St Basil's Cathedral in Red Square. I had been to the embassy once before, a few years earlier, at the end of a charity bike ride from St Petersburg to Moscow (which I undertook to mark the twentieth anniversary of the Russians dubbing my ma the 'Iron Lady'), when my fellow participants and I were invited to a reception. I don't think the staff had ever seen canapés disappear so quickly, such was the appetite we had built up during the long ride.

Incidentally, a few years ago I discovered the truth about the origin of that nickname. It arose from speech my mother made in 1976, strongly attacking the Soviet Union's ambition 'to become the most powerful imperial nation the world has seen . . . They put guns before butter, while we put just about everything before guns.' The speech was widely reported, and Yuriy Gavrilov, a young journalist for the Red Army's newspaper, the *Red Star*, had the idea of likening Mum to Germany's 'Iron Chancellor', Otto von Bismarck. It was an inspired idea: the name has stuck to her ever since. I read the tale in a newspaper interview with Gavrilov, and was delighted to learn the truth. There was another interesting quote, too. 'I always found her attractive as a woman,' said Gavrilov. 'If I hadn't, maybe I would have used a harsher label to describe her. She was possessed of a kind of atristocractic beauty.'

I think it was during the general election that followed Mum's resignation that it really sank in for me how different life would be. Now that she was no longer an MP but Baroness Thatcher, we were all abruptly and unexpectedly cut off from all the pantomime of politics and electioneering. I was no longer glued to the television. Polling days became like any other. We were off the hook as far as manifestos, rogue polls, wobbly Thursdays and other electoral tests were concerned. Our time was up. But the painful manner of my mother's ousting was all too raw for her, or us, to yet look back on elections with a mellow attitude or regard them as a rich vein of illuminating and amusing anecdotes to come. After thirty-three years in the House of Commons, thirty-one of them on the front bench, Mum described the events leading to her forced resignation as 'treachery with a smile on its face'.

Soon she wasn't even the last prime minister but the last-but-one. Then, in the final years of the last century and the beginning of this one, Conservative leadership elections filled the newspapers with musical-chairs regularity – some might claim monotony. The day of one of the leadership votes, between Kenneth Clarke and numerous other contestants (she came out in support of Iain Duncan-Smith), I offered to take her to lunch at the Ritz in Piccadilly. I thought she might be feeling maudlin about the whole thing, and rather out of the action. I memorised a list of jollier topics to get us through lunch.

I needn't have bothered. The restaurant that day resembled the Members' Dining Room in the House of Commons, as old colleagues almost formed a queue to have a chat. One Eurosceptic told her, 'Margaret, you know what this leadership election is all about?' (This was a novelty for my mother who had been in the business of lecturing others for so long.) He continued, 'People are calling it: ABC – anyone but Clarke.'

My mother was writing another book, this one entitled *Statecraft: Strategies for a Changing World*, and was keen to discuss it with old friends. Her chapters on Europe would cause particular controversy, as she called for a renegotiation of UK membership to preserve sovereignty, but then she had never been shy of speaking her mind.

Now that I live in south London, I've always assumed that with Thatcher as my surname no one would bother sending me political literature. Until, that is, one Blair election, when I opened a letter from Kirsty McNeil, the Labour parliamentary candidate for North Southwark and Bermondsey.

'*Dear Carol Thatcher*,' it began, '*I am writing to ask for your support so that I can make a difference to our community. Labour's investment in our community has resulted in three hundred and forty extra teachers . . .*' and so it went on.

The best bit was the printed 'handwritten' PS, which read: '*If you want a Labour poster for your window please get in touch with me at the address above.'*

As I live on the eighth floor of a block of flats, the only floating voter likely to catch a glimpse of such a poster would be a passenger in the window seat of an aircraft flying downriver on the approach to London's City airport. Even then he or she would have to be armed with a pretty decent pair of binoculars. I chuckled at the sheer lunacy of the letter, before toying fleetingly with the idea of ringing the campaign hotline and ordering a couple of Labour posters to be delivered to a Thatcher.

Crawfie, my ma's PA, had the best take on the whole political process. 'Don't look back,' she said, as she'd often said before. 'You're not going there.'

It's a slogan I still wholeheartedly embrace.

Chapter Twelve

UPSTREAM

I LEARNED EVERYTHING I know about surviving in the political goldfish bowl from Dad. He turned in an Oscar-winning performance in a supporting role he never even auditioned for. Future spouses – however much the goal posts may move – could do worse than take him as their role model. His courtesy, his sportsman's sense of fair play and his glorious sense of humour served well to the end of his Downing Street days.

Towards the end of his spell at Number Ten, Dad received a letter from an American who was seeking advice on how to approach the role of consort as his wife had just been made the president of the local riding club.

Dad's reply to 'Mr Connecticut' was vintage Denis:

Thank you for your letter of May 6 which I return for easy reference. I am unsure whether there is a similarity of scope or scale of being the spouse of the President of the Riding Club with that of being the spouse of the Prime Minister of the United Kingdom. The following guidelines, which are not in order of priority, may be of operational assistance to you:

a) Never ever talk to the press, local or national. A smiling 'Good Morning' will suffice. Remember that it is better to keep your mouth shut and be thought a fool than open it and remove all doubt. Avoid telling them to 'sod off'; it makes them cross.

b) Never ever appear speaking on TV. This is the short cut to disaster.

c) Never make speeches longer than four minutes, and prepare them very carefully to ensure that there is no possible quote. This results in the press not even reporting that you were there at all.

d) When visiting or opening factories, i.e. horse shoe manufacturers, saddle makers, animal feeds, etc., take the elementary precaution of reading their last Annual Report so you know what sort of corporation it is and whether it makes any money, then you can ask moderately intelligent or tactful questions.

e) When Members of the Club approach you with complaints and suggestions as to the conduct thereof, listen attentively and then say 'I will pass on your excellent comments' and then forget it . . .

f) Avoid the small function wherever possible. The Annual Picnic for the Stable Boys on Lincoln's Birthday can be deadly. Carry hipflask so you can lace the Coca-Cola but don't get caught doing it.

g) Avoid any possible 'run in' with the police or FBI, as this tends to attract unfavourable comment.

The price of keeping moderately trouble free is everlasting vigilance and the strict observance of the above rules of the game.

Good Luck and good wishes,

Denis Thatcher

A big slice of the Maggie Thatcher story would be missing if my father's contribution were overlooked. While my mother was PM, one of the questions I was asked most often was 'What was it like to be Denis?' And let's not forget that it was her husband's surname, not hers, that Mum elevated into a dictionary term. 'Thatcherism,' according to the *Oxford English Dictionary*, means: 'The political and economic policies advocated by Margaret Hilda Thatcher.'

Dad had never given interviews to the press, in line with his advice to 'Mr Connecticut' and when I'd pulled family strings to have a chat with him for an affectionate piece in the *Daily Telegraph* to mark his seventieth birthday, I'm afraid I hadn't helped the journalistic cause.

What, I asked him, was his recipe for septuagenarian fitness?

'Gin and cigarettes,' he replied instantly, an answer which appeared in the newspaper. Sackfuls of letters were subsequently hauled up to his study in the flat atop Number Ten, most of them from correspondents either protesting what a bad example he was to the young generation, or suggesting that he should be more onside with booze lobbies.

After that experience, he understandably took some persuading to sanction an authorised biography, but he did eventually agree, even providing a list of friends and contacts to whom I could speak. Gleefully, I set off with my tape recorder to get to know my father via the role of biographer. Fortunately, Dad began to take to the idea and allowed me to interview him as well. He proved a pleasure to work with. A mutual friend who regularly lunched with Dad told me that my father had confided that when he woke up on a morning when I'd be turning up for more research on the DT cv, he genuinely looked forward to it.

The title of the book came easily. Guests arriving at receptions at Number Ten often (especially when the going was rough) asked Dad how he was faring. 'You know me,' he'd reply. 'I just keep my head below the parapet.' Those final three words summed up the secret of his survival in the goldfish bowl.

To find out how my father compared to other consorts, I decided to investigate the species. Their role interested me because though in theory it's dead easy – smile on the red carpet, lap up the perks – in fact there's far more to it than that. But there were few sources of information. In the twentieth century only three women before Mum had risen to lead a nation, and all were widows by the time they came to power so there was no one to tell me about being a male consort. The original 'Iron Lady', Golda Meir of Israel, was widowed almost twenty years before she was elected prime minister; the husband of Sirimavo Bandaranaike of Ceylon (now Sri Lanka) was assassinated the year before her election; and Indira Gandhi, India's first and (so far) only female prime minister, lost her husband six years before she came to power.

Having met Mrs Gandhi, I was particularly interested in how her husband, Feroze, had coped. For marrying the daughter of India's first prime minister, Panjit Nehru, Feroze was mercilessly dubbed 'the nation's son-in-law'. Nehru was also frosty towards him, believing that Indira had married beneath her. After a romantic beginning – Feroze proposed on the steps of the Sacré-Coeur Basilica in Paris – the pair quarrelled both politically and personally, and for a while they split up, although they were reconciled after he suffered his first heart attack. He died a year later, at the age of only forty-eight, leaving two sons, Rajiv and Sanjay, both of whom were also destined to die young.

The wife of Scott of the Antarctic was another famous spouse who intrigued me. Robert Falcon Scott had married the bohemian and rather sophisticated Kathleen Bruce in 1908. They inhabited completely different worlds. A talented sculptress, and friend to Rodin and Isadora Duncan, Kathleen transformed herself into the perfect, self-sacrificing explorer's wife. When she waved farewell in New Zealand as Scott left for that ill-fated race to the South Pole against Amundsen, she said: 'I decided not to say goodbye to my man because I didn't want anyone to see him look sad.' On the strain of waiting, she wrote, 'All these long weary days with no news.' When she eventually received confirmation of her husband's death she had already been a widow for a year. How deep she must have dug to tap the reserves of emotional and artistic energy to sculpt the two fine statues of her husband, one of which still stands in Waterloo Place, just off London's Pall Mall.

By no means all consorts were so self-sacrificing. Both Carmen Franco of Spain and Eva Perón of Argentina were acquisitive, diamond-loving women, though they hailed from totally different backgrounds. Eva, better known as Evita, was born out of wedlock to a peasant mother, while Carmen had aristocratic Spanish parents who were so opposed to their teenage daughter's proposed marriage to Spain's most decorated soldier and future military dictator that they likened it to allowing her to marry a bullfighter.

Carmen became the most influential woman in Spain, and was dubbed 'Doña Collares' for the pearl necklaces that became her trademark. Jewellers in Madrid resorted to establishing an unofficial insurance syndicate to indemnify themselves against her voracious sweeps of their shops during which she made off with any baubles she fancied. Gratis, obviously.

In 1947 Eva Perón paid a high-profile state visit to Spain as part of her 'Rainbow Tour' of Europe, meeting various heads of state.

One of General Franco's biographers, Paul Preston, observed that a fashion contest quickly developed between the two first ladies. 'The most often flourished weapons were extravagant hats. The victory went to the Argentinian.'

Carmen Franco outlived her husband and survived to a lonely old age, having suffered a series of tragedies and witnessed the disintegration of her family. Eva Perón died of cancer at the age of thirty-three, having been hailed as the 'Spiritual Leader of the Nation'. She was given a state funeral. Her husband, Juan, survived her for twenty years and his third wife, Isabel, went on to become the first female head of state in the world.

Then there was Jiang Qing, the fourth wife of Chinese communist leader Mao Zedong. A thrice-married former actress who went by the stage name of 'Blue Apple', she was Chairman Mao's political partner during the disastrous Cultural Revolution, becoming a member of the Politburo and deputy director of the Revolution. Jiang tolerated Mao's endless womanising, and described herself as Mao's dog. 'I bit whomever he asked me to bite.' She exhibited the double standards of many other dictators' wives, living in the lap of luxury herself – she had her silk underwear ironed – while the people starved – and even harboured delusions that she was Empress Wu Zetian, an empress of the Tang dynasty and the only woman in the history of China to assume the title Empress Regnant. After Mao's death Jiang led the radical political group known as the Gang of Four. She was sentenced to death after the Four's downfall, although that was later commuted to life imprisonment. After developing cancer, she committed suicide in 1991.

Margaret Truman, daughter of President Harry Truman, wrote a book about the role of America's First Lady, in which she said, *'The job remains undefined, frequently misunderstood and subject to political attacks far worse in some ways than those any President has ever faced.'* Of course, the role of consort has moved with the times. In the United States, Bill Clinton went from being president to almost becoming the first male 'First Lady' when his wife Hillary was elected senator for New York and almost became America's first woman president. Norma Major stamped her dignity and personality on the British role from 1990 to 1997, and then along came Cherie Blair, and now Sarah Brown.

The experiences of their predecessors can hardly have been encouraging. Jim Callaghan's wife, Audrey (a politician and campaigner in her own right), shunned the limelight and did not enjoy life in Number Ten, Ted Heath remained unmarried, and the admirably independent Mary Wilson, wife of Harold, disliked the place so much that she refused to live there. Before I embarked on the first draft of *Below the Parapet*, I read an interview with Lady Wilson, who had featured as Gladys in 'Mrs Wilson's Diary' in *Private Eye*. 'It was a joke,' she said. 'I used to read it and think what [they'd] described wasn't nearly as bizarre as it really was. I could have told ... some things which were much funnier.' Real style on Mary's part, I thought. She continued, 'I wasn't brought up to make fun of people. And I don't think it's very nice. All right, if you can't stand the heat, keep out of the kitchen and all that, but then one is in the kitchen because one happens to be involved with the person who's doing the job.' There, in a nutshell, is the conundrum of the modern political consort.

Having satirised Mary Wilson, *Private Eye* did the same for my father. Until then he had been widely thought of as 'invisible' by the world's press, as Mum took centre stage. At one early party conference, a journalist from the *Evening Standard* observed, 'Mr Denis Thatcher is still fighting shy of playing the role of full-time consort to Margaret.' Inherently shy, Dad had deliberately kept out of the limelight and was keen to do nothing to overshadow or jeopardise the future of his famous wife.

John Wells, actor, writer and co-founder of *Private Eye*, who wrote 'Mrs Wilson's Diary', turned his attention to Dad when Mum became leader of the Conservative Party. He spotted Dad at the back of the celebrations, 'grinning very widely – obviously he'd had a few – and the television lights reflected off his glasses. He immediately seemed to me to be a very attractive comic character; a really charming saloon bar figure . . . there was something very theatrical about his appearance . . . straight away, I thought he was a well-drawn, possible Wodehouseian figure.'

After the general election, it was decided that, rather than another diary, Wells should write letters from Dad to a fictitious golfing pal called Bill (modelled on Bill Deedes, one-time cabinet minister, former editor of the *Daily Telegraph*, and one of Dad's closest friends). The first 'Dear Bill' appeared on 15 May 1979, two weeks after Mum became PM. It read:

Dear Bill,

So sorry I couldn't make it on Tuesday . . . M. insisted I turn up for some kind of State Opening of Parliament or other. I had assumed now the election was over I would be excused this kind of thing, but oh no. I had just carried my spare clubs out to the jalopy when heigh-ho! – up goes a window and M. is giving me my marching orders. It's off to Moss Bros. for the full kit, and at that moment, I don't mind telling you I couldn't help thinking pretty enviously of you, Monty and the Major enjoying a few pre-match snifters at the nineteenth without a care in the world . . .

[At the House of Commons] M. then had to go off to do her stuff so I just mooched around for a while, looking for a watering hole. What a place, Bill! If you ask me, it's just an antiquated rabbit warren – miles and miles of corridors, with chaps in evening dress wandering about like a lot of superannuated penguins. Luckily I bumped into a familiar face in the shape of George Brown. He seemed to know his way about and we ended up in a nice little bar overlooking the river, with an awfully jolly crowd of chaps who were watching the show on the TV.

It all seemed to go quite smoothly, but I was a bit miffed to see M. fussing over that fellow [Norman St John] Stevas, and taking the fluff off his collar. To tell you the truth, I don't like the cut of that chap's jib. If you ask me, he's not absolutely 100 per cent and when I said as much a lot of the fellows at the bar agreed.

Must close, as M. has got some Hun coming to dinner and I've got to do my stuff again. I sometimes wonder who won the bloody war!

Yours aye!

Denis

John Wells and Richard Ingram, the *Eye*'s editor, soon twigged that gin and golf were to Dad as shoes were to Imelda Marcos. As more letters were published, Dad's so-called 'character' developed: he was a boozing, smoking, sports-mad male chauvinist married to a domineering wife (referred to as 'She Who Must Be Obeyed' or the 'Boss') and deserved the sympathy of all red-blooded men. The letters were very successful and soon became one of the most widely read features of the magazine. Even Dad became a keen reader, chiefly because friends thought he was ghosting them, and he admitted they often got it right on anything from his tirades against the 'filthy reptiles of Fleet Street' to his political incorrectness on matters of foreign affairs, or his views on the 'pinkoes and traitors' running the BBC. They even picked up some of his peculiar turns of phrase, such as that hotels 'charged like the Light Brigade'.

Dad's amusement at the letters began to wane a little when they were published in paperback and fans started to send copies to Downing Street for him to sign, expecting him to pay the return postage. Or when a television company commissioned a poster showing him dressed in a pinny and plastered it over every London Underground station that Dad seemed to frequent.

Worse still, after John Wells appeared in wig and make-up as Dad to read some of the letters on a TV chat show, the role morphed into a stage play entitled *Anyone for Denis*, which opened in London in May 1981. Dad found the play highly offensive, especially when it portrayed him as being so drunk at Chequers that he couldn't tell the difference between a urine sample and a glass of whisky. I was asked to review the play for the *News of the World* and said that, while the letters were funny and affectionate, the play opened him to ridicule.

Poor Dad was dragged along with Mum to a charity performance of the play a few weeks later, on the basis it would show they were 'good sports'. They even had to host a reception for the cast at Number Ten, but they managed to hide their annoyance well on both occasions. The whole exercise could have backfired dreadfully and neither of my parents was amused, but fortunately they were hailed in the press the following day as showing great humour and being able to laugh at themselves, so the situation was saved.

The influence of the 'Dear Bill' letters turned out to be a gift. Just as the 'Iron Lady' soubriquet had done wonders for Mum, 'Dear Bill' brought Dad into the public consciousness. His mailbag quadrupled, because eager correspondents hoped that writing to him could be the back-door route to the prime minister. Sitting in his study each morning after breakfast with his fountain pen, Dad tackled each one personally, refusing to shunt them along to the correspondence department. At the peak of his popularity, he averaged at least fifty replies a week. Explaining his decision to me later, he said, 'I decided it was better to do it this way rather than just sending out a printed reply. I thought it was more useful than the party's point of view – i.e. Margaret's point of view. The very difficult ones I sent down to the political office, but after a time you got a feel as to whether they [the writers] were on your side or whether they were digging up information to possibly use against the prime minister. You had to use a bit of common sense and read between the lines.'

In a similar attempt to keep in contact with voters and fans, Dad liked to 'work the other side of the street' to Mum on walkabouts, giving those with little chance of seeing her at least the opportunity to see or talk to him, so that they didn't go home from the rally, supermarket opening or speech empty-handed, so to speak.

Although consistently over the top, the 'Dear Bill' letters became increasingly affectionate towards Dad and soon turned him into a respected national institution. Although he was unwilling to admit it, once he became more confident as prime ministerial consort he even began to play up to the image *Private Eye* had given him.

At a Tory party reception for the faithful, a blue-rinsed lady approached him and said discreetly, 'Mr Thatcher, I hear you have a drink problem.'

Dad went for it, waving his empty glass theatrically and declaring loudly, 'Yes, Madam. I have. There is never enough of it.'

And at a charity luncheon, a member of the public pressed my eternally polite and courteous father on exactly what he *did* all day while his wife was working all hours running the country. Dad paused and then informed his inquisitor, 'When I'm not totally pissed, I like to play a round or two of golf.'

Almost immediately after my mother left office, Dad was awarded a hereditary baronetcy – the first such honour to be granted since the 1960s and the last British hereditary honour to be granted to anyone outside the royal family. He was now Sir Denis Thatcher, first Baronet of Scotney in the County of Kent, and none, in my opinion, deserved it more. (He chose Scotney because he was born in Kent, had served in a Kentish regiment, and had always felt our time in the county had been our happiest.) On his death the title would go to Mark. I became the Honourable Carol Thatcher, not that I ever used it. Many years later when I arrived at a hotel in Singapore, a friend had upgraded me to a better room. Without my knowledge, I had been re-registered as 'The Honourable Carol Thatcher'. I was fulsomely welcomed at reception and handed my key card.

'Should I call you Judge?' enquired the charming girl who

escorted me to my room. I had just flown in from Sydney and wondered whether in my tiredness I was missing something. As I looked down at the welcome folder I could see why. In bold type were the words, 'Judge Thatcher Carol Jane'. The 'Honourable' had somehow morphed into 'Your Honour' and then 'Judge'. I wondered what those meticulous protocol gurus at *Debrett's* would have made of it.

The Queen bestowed on Mum the Order of Merit, one of the nation's highest honours. There was some debate about whether she should accept a hereditary or life peerage, but she eventually opted for the second. I breathed a sigh of relief. If she'd accepted the former, I would have automatically become Lady Carol. An acquaintance who was expert at anagrams told me gleefully that Lady Carol was an anagram of 'A Racy Doll'. I was thrilled; how I would have liked, indeed relished an innings in that party mode, but Lady Carol Thatcher was infinitely less glamorous: a chatter char dolly.

Mum's decision fortunately spared me the nearly impossible challenge of becoming ladylike and acquiring attributes such as manners, decorum and dress sense appropriate to the rank. Years before, when I'd lived as a young journalist in Sydney I had appeared on some minor Worst Dressed List. When a reporter called for my reaction, I got myself off the hook by claiming to be confused: 'Next year, am I meant to try and move up or down it?'

The *Evening Standard* asked me to write a piece about my reaction to my mother's elevation from Mrs Thatcher to Baroness

Thatcher of Kesteven (later she was promoted to the Order of the Garter, Britain's highest order of chivalry). I concluded by saying that I was the only girl in the world who would ever be able to say that my mother had been Britain's first female prime minister, and that was honour enough for me. I meant it.

But it was also an enormous honour to be my father's daughter, as I soon discovered when giving lunch or dinner speeches and being asked for Denis anecdotes. There remained among my parents' generation a curiosity about what it was like to be 'Maggie' and 'Denis'. If pressed on this subject, Dad had two stories he dusted off for public consumption. I often had to authenticate them as I went around the London social scene.

The first was about when the PM's office despatched him on consort duty down to Bristol. The travel arrangements were a bit haphazard, and when Dad got to Paddington he found out that no one had reserved him a seat on a very crowded train. Dad wandered up and down the corridor – it was an old-fashioned train with separate compartments – and eventually found an empty compartment. Pleased to be able to sit down and immerse himself in the *Daily Telegraph*, he didn't give the notice on the door a second thought. It read, 'Reserved for Rosewood Psychiatric Hospital.'

All was calm until when the train stopped at Reading and the patients were ushered in. Dad said, 'All these chaps piled into the carriage, shepherded by a very young, nervous-looking male nurse. He got them settled in and started to count them,

"One, two, three, four . . .' Then he got to me and said, "Who are you?"

'I'm the prime minister's husband,' I said.

"Five, six, seven, eight, nine . . .'

On another occasion, Dad decided to skive off out of Number Ten for a golfing weekend. He surreptitiously slipped out by crossing the rose garden and ducking through a back door which opened onto Horse Guards Parade. He jumped into his car and headed off down the motorway, clubs in the back, delighted at the prospect of zero official duties, several rounds of golf, and copious drinks at the nineteenth hole. Then he realised that in his haste he had left his jacket - containing his wallet, credit cards, cheque book and cash in the inside pocket - hanging over the back of his chair in his study.

Ah well, he thought, his golfing pals would be good for a loan. The problem was they were some way down the track and the fuel gauge was plummeting towards empty. Dad made it as far as Honiton in Devon, where he found a branch of his bank, an establishment he had banked with for donkey's years.

'May I see the manager?' he asked.

'The manager is on leave.'

'The assistant manager?'

'Why?'

Dad opted for some rank-pulling. 'My name is Denis Thatcher. I am the prime minister's husband. I have left my wallet in my jacket in Number Ten Downing Street and I need some cash.'

He got a 'Nice try, sir' look from the young man – who was clearly destined for a glittering future in banking. Dad scowled. 'You don't look like your photograph,' he was informed, which didn't help his cause. Then, when asked if he could recite his regular standing orders, he failed the test (as if anyone can).

Eventually the weary young employee reluctantly agreed to advance Dad £50, not the £100 Dad was after. 'So much for being the prime minister's husband,' he ended the tale.

Publication of *Below the Parapet* was scheduled for April 1996. In the countdown I had the idea of playing to Dad's gin-and-golfing image by asking United Distillers – makers of Gordon's Gin – if we could have some of the outsized cardboard cutouts and a few bottles for the book launch, to underline that Denis and gin were as inseparably twinned as Maggie and her handbags. The reply surprised me. The powers-that-be at United said that Denis and his fictitious golfing pals in 'Dear Bill' were too ancient and fuddy-duddy for the younger image they wanted to spin in modern times. Their decision rather backfired on them, as the newspapers loved the story. On the basis that no publicity is bad publicity, both gin and my book were on the front pages for three consecutive days. The *Daily Telegraph* went to town with a piece entitled, 'Dear Bill, Those Gordon's chaps say gin and me don't mix.' The article said, 'The country's biggest gin producer, Gordon's, has snubbed Britain's most famous gin drinker, Sir Denis Thatcher. It has refused a request by his daughter, Carol, to provide free snifters for the launch of a biography she has written about him ... A company memorandum leaked to The *Daily Telegraph* says: "This would take us back to the dark ages."'

The week the book was published, I was so nervous about the reviews that I bought the relevant newspapers at South Kensington Tube station and headed straight to a bar in the Fulham Road. Fortified by a spicy Bloody Mary, I read them and was mightily relieved. They were good – both about Dad and about the biography. Rather chuffed, I hopped on the Tube and went to my parents' new home in Chester Square, Belgravia. My mother was on a speaking tour in the United States but Dad was home and had been combing the reviews, too. He was pleased for me, especially with the comment: 'Thatcher has done her homework.'

United Distillers kindly capitulated and gave us both gin and whisky for a spirited launch party at the East India Club in St James's Square. My mother had generously said Dad and I could give a small dinner party in her office afterwards. We did, and when Mum rang to check all was going well, we were all making so much noise no one heard the telephone.

My subsequent publicity tour had echoes of a general election campaign: criss-crossing the country, only this time with the aim of signing and selling books rather than canvassing for votes. One of my first ports of call was the BBC for a live interview on *Today* with Sue MacGregor. I regularly listened to and admired Sue, who had been an energetic trailblazer for women on the airwaves. Shortly after my mother became leader of the opposition Sue had interviewed her on *Woman's Hour*. Sue had a reputation for her schoolmarmly voice and my mother's had already been dubbed strident. The new leader apparently enquired of her interviewer, 'Will our voices sound rather similar?'

My voice wasn't my worry – rather the thoroughness of *Today's* researchers on my book. Sue greeted me with her copy of *Below the Parapet* open at page 229, in which I had written of a marathon speech given by President Banda of Malawi and attended by my parents. Quoting my father, I'd written: 'I looked around and Margaret had gone – chin on chest, fast asleep. Bernard Ingham was slumped on the table snoring, Charles Powell fast asleep with his eyes open. But they didn't get me; I used the old army trick – finger touching roof of mouth and if you fall asleep you're either sick or wake up.'

Unfortunately, when I came to look at the text again, I found that I had written 'President Panda'. My reaction was one of comprehensive blind panic. One typo and I had turned the autocratic Dr Hastings Kamuzu Banda – who in 1971 had declared himself President for Life – into a bamboo-chomping animal ambassador of China. Fortunately, I was able to get my mistake corrected in the paperback edition.

The book was flying off the shelves and the responses had been largely positive. I received a number of gratifying letters from readers of *Below the Parapet*, including one from the television personality Esther Rantzen. 'You bring him to life with such warmth and reality – while at the same time painting a picture of his lifestyle with your mother that is affectionate and sharp,' she wrote.

A ninety-two-year-old from London wrote, 'Everyone knows your mother was a remarkable woman – thank you for introducing us to your very remarkable father.'

My publicity tour had me speaking at a Foyles literary lunch in London, another for the *Yorkshire Post* in Harrogate, signing books in Waterstone's, Manchester, and giving myriad interviews to fellow reptiles. I had just finished an informal signing session at a bookshop in the City of London when the publicist took a phone call and told me some great news: '*Below the Parapet* is number three on the bestseller list.'

I whooped with excitement and immediately called Crawfie in Mum's office to find out if Dad was there. He was. Crawfie promised to keep shtum and put some champagne on ice. I was scheduled to sign books at Blackwell's bookshop in Reading, followed by a literary dinner in Henley-on-Thames. My driver warned me that the traffic would be getting worse by the moment, so I could only afford a short pit-stop to communicate the good news to Dad. Rushing to his office, I found him at his desk.

'How's it all going?' he asked.

Unable to contain my excitement, I cried in triumph, 'We're number three on the bestseller list!'

Quick as a flash, he came back: 'Would that be fiction or non-fiction?'

Chapter Thirteen

AN OMINOUS CLOUD

I WELL REMEMBER THE moment it hit me that my mother's memory was no longer the extraordinary phenomenon it had been all my life. The realisation came as a thunderbolt.

It was the summer of 2000, and I had invited her to lunch at the Mandarin Oriental in Knightsbridge, overlooking Hyde Park. A friend had recommended the restaurant, and the hotel was geographically convenient for us both. In addition, she knew it when it had been the Hyde Park Hotel under the ownership of her friend Lord Forte. Having made the arrangement, Mum's office booked the reservation for me because the detectives who were now a permanent fixture of her life also had to be accommodated.

As an economy gesture on my behalf my mother insisted that we book into the coffee shop rather than the rather fancy restaurant. We settled into our seats and gazed out across Hyde Park, where joggers, pram pushers and cyclists were enjoying the gorgeous summer sunshine. It was such a rare 'mother and daughter' occasion, I relished it. Mum was hardly a 'lady who lunched', and I'd had to wait months to find a space in her diary when we could get together.

It's not always easy to make polite, lunch-time conversation with a mother who for decades has had world leaders and statesmen to engage with in meaningful and potentially world-changing talks. But we talked about various things, including the recent Concorde crash in Paris in which all one hundred and thirteen passengers and crew had perished. I had been a great fan of the supersonic aircraft, and said how much I'd always enjoyed watching its distinctive drop-nose arc over the skies above my little terraced house in Fulham after take-off from Heathrow; I used to nip out into the garden for a better view. We chuckled as I reminded her of the time when Dad, during a lunch at Chequers, had complained to a senior honcho at British Airways that on a flight back from New York he'd found Concorde noisy, bone-rattling and cramped. The guest fired back straight away. 'But Denis,' he said, 'it doesn't last long.'

Mum reminded me that the only time I had flown on Concorde had been on a trip with her to New York, when she was going on to a speaking engagement in Aspen, Colorado. She had begged me to buy a new, smart suitcase for the trip. I had thought such a purchase superfluous expenditure and instead packed all my stuff in a zip-up soft-sided number probably more appropriate for a camping trip. When we got off Concorde to change flights, my scruffy piece of baggage, priority labels dangling from its worn canvas handles, was the first down the luggage belt from the plane. A pained expression crossed Lady T's face.

Having ordered our lunch, I reminisced about the night she'd become party leader back in 1975. After finishing my law exam I'd walked through Hyde Park on my way home, wondering what the future would hold.

'Oh, how I wish I could do it all again,' she said, brightening at the mention of her stupendous victory. I guess you can get politicians out of politics but you can't get politics out of them.

Thoughts of Hyde Park prompted her back to the dreadful day in July 1982 when she had been chairing a meeting in the Cabinet Office, and heard and felt what she immediately recognised as a bomb. In fact, it was two. One in Hyde Park, the other, simultaneously, in Regent's Park. The victims were the men and horses of the Household Cavalry and the band of the Royal Green Jackets. Eleven soldiers were killed, more than fifty people were injured, and seven horses were killed or had to be shot because of their injuries. The British public were profoundly appalled at the spectacle of the dead men and horses heaped in Hyde Park.

On a happier note, Mum was pleased to recall the last time

she'd had lunch overlooking Hyde Park, when she had managed to secure a window table with her beloved Texan grandson, Michael, and they'd enjoyed watching the mounted bands and other soldiers in full ceremonial attire returning to barracks after Trooping the Colour on Horse Guards Parade.

A mutual friend had recently told me that he'd been at a dinner party with my parents at which General Sir Michael Rose was the guest of honour. Rose, a former commander of the SAS, had also commanded the UN Protection Force in Bosnia in the mid-1990s.

'That must have been interesting?' I said.

'It was,' she replied.

Even though Mum had been out of office for ten years she still kept up to date with international events. It wasn't unusual to shift a pile of Sunday papers on the coffee table and find a paperback with a title like *Genocide in the Balkans*, its pages marked for research to incorporate into speeches to international organisations around the world.

I fully expected her to give me lengthy chapter and verse on Bosnia, and sat back, waiting for a characteristic monologue. But she soon became confused, and a few sentences later discussion of Bosnia had moved to the Falklands as she muddled up the Falkland conflict with the Yugoslav wars. You could have knocked me off my chair. Watching her struggle with her words and her memory, I simply couldn't believe it. She was in her seventy-fifth year, but I had always thought of her as ageless, timeless and one hundred per cent cast-iron damage-proof.

The contrast was all the more striking because, until that point, she'd always had a memory like a website. When she learned Latin at school she absorbed the vocabulary and declensions with her blotting-paper brain. It was a skill honed to perfection during her studies for her degree at Oxford, when all the scientific equations added yet another dimension to an already orderly mind. Then, when she read law and qualified as a barrister, her memory training was complete. By the time she entered politics she was famous for not just reading and analysing her briefs but virtually knowing them off by heart. During Prime Minister's Questions, she could rise from the front bench in an economic debate and recite the rate of inflation all the way back to William Gladstone without needing to refer to a note.

From the fateful day of our lunch, more clues began to emerge; tell-tale signs that something wasn't quite right. Whereas previously one never had to say anything to her twice, because she'd already filed it away in her formidable memory bank, Mum started asking the same questions over and over again, unaware that she was doing so. It might be something innocuous like 'What time is my car coming?' or 'When am I going to the hairdresser?' or 'What time is Denis coming home?' but the fact she needed to go on repeating them opened the page on a new and frightening chapter in our lives.

I had to learn to be patient; a quality I freely admit is in short supply. I also had to learn that she had an illness and that it wasn't personal. That's the worst thing about dementia: it gets you every time. Its sufferers look and act the same, but beneath the familiar exterior something quite different is going on. They're in another world, and you cannot enter. Much of my mother's daily life was affected. Timing became a particular concern. If I said, 'Oh, do relax, Mum. The car won't be here for ten minutes,' she'd jump up, hook her handbag over her arm and say, 'Ten minutes? I'll go down now,' as if I'd said thirty seconds.

Such memory loss often begins with short-term breakdown. I described this to a friend, who said, 'Carol, it must be awful for you.'

'That's not my worry,' I replied. 'I suspect it's immensely frustrating for her.'

On any visit, I'd first pop into the kitchen to scan the notice board where her calendar was written out, before going to see her in the sitting room. 'Hi, Mum,' I'd say, 'how was your lunch with so-and-so in the House of Lords? That must have been interesting.'

She'd look up as if she barely recognised me and say, 'Did I, darling?'

Her doctor recommended that she make no more public speeches on health grounds, a ban which she reluctantly observed. As she became increasingly frail, many of her friends and colleagues became extraordinarily considerate and loyal at dealing with the new Lady T. The woman who had dominated discussions for so long could no longer lead conversations or keep up with the thread of a drinks party conversation. On bad days, she could hardly remember the beginning of a sentence by the time she got to the end.

One night in March 2004, when I knew there were a couple of political colleagues coming for dinner, I grabbed a copy of the *Evening Standard* on the way to Mum's house. The headlines focused chiefly on the terrorist bombs that had killed a hundred and ninety-one people on the commuter trains into Madrid that day, and injured seventeen hundred others. I carefully tried to explain the story to Mum before her guests arrived, but when they did and asked, 'Margaret, if you were prime minister what would be the first action you would take?' all memory of the story had vanished from her mind.

Even though it was a subject which began to dominate my life, I couldn't bring myself to see such films as *Iris*, about novelist Iris Murdoch's slide into dementia, or *Away from Her*, starring Julie Christie as a Canadian septuagenarian who is in the early stages of Alzheimer's and moves into a care home. I had to remind myself that we were lucky, however. Friends of mine had to drop everything to race to opposite ends of the country to attend to ailing parents who suffered from the same darkness but who lived alone or without proper supervision. My mother would always have a driver and a twenty-four-hour police guard, not to mention enough funds to afford the appropriate nursing care.

Of course, there were flashes of Mum's old self every now and again, particularly when events from the past were mentioned. It was as if the dementia had actually sharpened her powers of long-term recall. Like most politicians, she still had good memories of her time at Number Ten. When I invited a friend round for tea once, he engaged her in conversation about Mikhail Gorbachev. Quick as a flash, she snapped back into Iron Lady mode and was utterly engaging. She even gave my friend the rundown of a stunning portrait done of her in her Garter robes which hangs in the Drawing Room.

It took us all time to realise that she couldn't remember a newspaper headline she had just read, or what she'd had for breakfast that morning. But when a friend asked, off-the-cuff, 'Oh, Margaret, do you remember rationing?' he got a full ten minutes of my mother's best grocer's daughter's tips on how to jazz up tinned Spam or powdered egg.

My mother hadn't mentioned her birthplace, Grantham, to me for many years until it started cropping up in sentences and I realised she now thought of it as her 'home'. It was a case of classic dementia, coupled with a series of mini-strokes. What was most galling was that there was nothing I could do: this cruel disease takes its own course. Thank goodness she still had Crawfie as her personal-assistant-cum-hairdresser-cum-general-dogsbody, and other loyal devotees around her, not to mention her marmalade rescue cat, Pussikins, which gave her great comfort.

I think her illness must have been especially hard on my father. I remember the night he took her out to Bill Deedes's ninetieth birthday party in 2003. They were both looking forward to congratulating a man who had been such a thread of wisdom and friendship throughout their lives. My mother had been given the table plan and the guest list in advance, and was scheduled to sit next to Conrad Black, then proprietor of the *Daily Telegraph*.

'What shall I talk to him about?' she asked me.

'Look, Mum, you know him,' I reminded her, 'and you may not be able to get a word in edgeways.'

As Mum and Dad left, I said to my father anxiously, 'Oh, do look after her.'

My father smiled. ''Course I will, love. Been doing it for over fifty years.'

Neither of my parents handled each other's old age and ailing health terribly well. In early 2003, Dad decided to go on an extended trip to South Africa, which he had loved all his life. As a precaution, and because he was eighty-eight and getting a little breathless, his doctor gave him a check-up. An irregular heart murmur was detected, and before we knew it he was booked in for major heart surgery. Characteristically, the minute Dad was out of hospital – ten days after a six-hour heart bypass operation – he set himself a rigorous convalescence schedule, determined to get well enough to make his (now delayed) trip.

He checked into a country-house hotel on the edge of the New Forest to recuperate, and I went to visit him. As we went into the restaurant for lunch, the *maitre d'* told me how much they admired Dad, because when he first arrived he'd needed a walking stick to get across the room and now he could manage without. He'd worked so hard to get a little bit better and walk a bit further each day. Between courses, Dad directed my attention beyond the meticulously tended lawns to the personal exercise circuit he had devised for himself, adding some steps there and then another little circuit. I just hoped that, at his age, I would have his motivation, spirit and discipline.

True to his plan, two months after his operation Dad went to South Africa, where my brother was living, and Mark took him to Victoria Falls and other places my father hadn't been to for many years. He had a marvellous trip down memory lane. When asked, I publicly stated that his remarkable recovery must be down to 'copious gin-drinking'.

The first time I saw him on his return, I found him in the sitting room of his London home. 'Hi, Dad,' I said, thrilled to see him looking so tanned and well and relaxed.

'Sorry, Carol Jane,' he said, 'can't get up to greet you. Bit of a problem with my knees.'

'Oh, what a bore!' I cried. 'What about physiotherapy?'

'No,' said Dad. 'I'm going to see the doc about replacement kneecaps.'

'What?' I spluttered. 'You've just had major heart surgery. What is this? Your year for new spare parts?'

He laughed.

What none of us knew was that he was within a few weeks of the end. Soon afterwards he was again taken to hospital, and pancreatic cancer was diagnosed. He died on 23 June. We were all by his bedside. The Union Flag at Conservative Central Office was lowered as a mark of respect. His death was a huge shock, but when I look back I am grateful that it was mercifully quick.

Losing Dad was truly awful for Mum, not least because her dementia meant she kept forgetting he was dead, and I had to keep on giving her the bad news over and over again. It was very upsetting for us both. Every time it finally sank in that she had lost her husband of more than fifty years, she'd look at me sadly and say, 'Oh,' as I struggled to compose myself. 'Were we all there?' she'd ask softly.

Dad's funeral was on a glorious summer's day in the chapel designed by Christopher Wren at the Royal Hospital, Chelsea, where my parents had been frequent Sunday worshippers. 'The Last Post' was played by a bugler from Dad's old regiment, and even the top military brass said it was note perfect. A dozen Chelsea pensioners formed a guard of honour as Dad's coffin was carried from the chapel. Asked by journalists how it went, I said, 'It is very sad. But the litmus test of a funeral is whether the deceased would have approved, and he would have been very comforted by this.' The police escort to the crematorium in south-west London removed their helmets when we arrived, in a touching gesture of farewell. Dad would have been honoured.

Three months later, a memorial service for six hundred friends and family – including at least ten former cabinet ministers – was held at the Guards Chapel in Wellington Barracks. Bill Deedes described Dad as 'a vast improvement on the *Private Eye* model', adding, 'a lot more than golf and gin and funny friends went into the making of that Denis Thatcher'. My fourteen-year-old nephew, Michael, read one of Dad's favourite Bible passages, and we all posed for a family photograph on the steps afterwards; images of my mother's tearful face dominated the next day's newspapers.

My mother once said of my father, 'I could never have been prime minister for more than eleven years without Denis by my side ... He was a fund of shrewd advice and penetrating comment. And he very sensibly saved these for me rather than the outside world ... Being prime minister is a lonely job. In a sense, it ought to be – you cannot lead from a crowd. But with Denis there I was never alone. What a man, what a husband, what a friend.'

Tony Blair said: 'Sir Denis was a kind and generous-hearted man, a real gentleman, who had many friends here and abroad.'

Dad would have had a last chuckle at some of the headlines in the papers that accompanied his obituaries, for example the *Daily Telegraph*'s, which said, 'Dear Bill, Last Orders at the 19th. Buggeration.' The BBC reported that my father's motto was that prime minister's consorts should be 'Always present, never there.'

On my loo wall at home, outnumbered heavily by cartoons starring my mother, is just one remembering Dad, but it's probably the one I treasure the most. It's a cartoon from the *Daily Mail* featuring a fictional tombstone for my father with the words, 'Gone to the 19th hole.'

It makes me smile every time.

Chapter Fourteen

TROPICAL FISH

O<small>N</small> 25 A<small>UGUST</small> 2004, I was watching the early-morning reports from the Athens Olympics on the television in the flat I rent in Klosters, Switzerland, when the phone rang. I picked it up and a reporter from BBC Radio Four's *Today* programme asked, 'Can we have your reaction?'

'To what?' I asked cautiously. Getting family news via the media had been the story of my life.

'To the arrest of your brother in South Africa on charges of attempting to organise a coup in Equatorial New Guinea?'

I nearly choked. 'Equatorial where?' One develops pretty good shock absorbers being a prime minister's daughter, but this threw me totally off balance. Having established we weren't on air, I said, quite truthfully, that this was the first I'd heard of it and I had no idea whether my mother had been told or not because she was in the United States. I put the phone down, reeling.

I was already planning to fly home that day, so set about gathering up a few belongings while wondering what on earth this was all about. Because of the time difference, it was still too early to call my mother's PA in the States. A Swiss friend who was watching television called me to say the Mark story was massive. 'It's on every channel,' he warned.

I went to my computer and Googled 'Equatorial New Guinea', deciding that I at least ought to know where it was. I discovered it was a former Spanish colony which was now Africa's third biggest producer of oil. I switched on the television and saw reporters gathering outside Mark's house in Cape Town.

Having a drink at the bar at Zurich airport while I waited for my flight, I asked the young man next to me where he was from. 'South Africa,' he replied. 'And you?'

'London,' I said.

'Oh,' he said, 'your former prime minister's son has just been arrested for some coup.'

I whipped my boarding pass and passport off the bar and sat on them.

I'd been Maggie Thatcher's Daughter my whole life. Could I now cope with being Mark Thatcher's Sister as well?

Arriving at Heathrow, I was able to tell waiting reporters that I hadn't been able to speak to Mark or my mother, but my concern was about how worried my mother would be. I was speaking the truth. Later, after Mark had narrowly avoided prison and been fined £265,000, with a suspended prison sentence, after he admitted he'd been involved in buying a helicopter gunship for use in the alleged plot, I gave a frank interview to the *Daily Mail*. 'I was dismayed at the hurt and worry Mum was suffering because of Mark's involvement in the Equatorial Guinea plot,' I said. 'I was annoyed with my brother for getting embroiled in it, but my main concern was our mother . . . I know how terribly it worried her . . . In her state of health it was far from helpful to have such a nagging anxiety always at the back of her mind.'

Given my upbringing you'd think I'd have learned a thing or two about polarised reactions. Not so, or at least not until I started canvassing my friends on whether or not I should participate in a popular reality television show called *I'm a Celebrity . . . Get Me out of Here*.

The premise of the show is that a number of 'celebrities' are dropped into a camp in the jungle of Queensland, Australia, and left to fend for themselves, while an average of eleven million viewers watch night and day and gradually vote them out one by one. Oh, and the public also gets to vote on which 'celeb' gets to endure a daily challenge or 'Bushtucker Trial' to win food and basic essentials. These trials can range from eating some indigenous delicacy (usually vile and wriggling), to being buried alive or sharing a cave with a few more unsavoury creatures.

The show is presented by the diminutive Ant and Dec, and previous contestants included Tony Blackburn, Paul Burrell, Katie Price, Phil Tufnell, Janet Street-Porter, Kerry Katona and Joe Pasquale.

My friends either loved or loathed the idea. 'You've really gone looney this time' summed up the attitude of the first friend I tried out, whereas the second encouraged me to 'Go for it.'

Strangely, when I was first approached about participating, I didn't run a mile. I regarded it as an offer not to be refused. It was two years after my father's death and if I had learned one thing from losing him so suddenly, it was that I should start living for the moment.

For a start, I'd spent four of the best years of my life in Australia – although, admittedly, far closer to the watering holes overlooking Sydney harbour than our jungle camp was ever going to be. I also believe adventures and opportunities are not frequent visitors once you reach the wrong side of fifty. And when it came to travelling overseas I'd always favoured the wacky, rather than the conventional. The idea of a mix of *Crocodile Dundee* and *Neighbours* held a strange appeal.

Having followed the advice of the second camp and agreed to go though, I, too, began to have my doubts. The day I had to sign on the dotted line, there was definitely a moment when I nearly turned and fled. As I waited in my agent's reception, I spotted some photographs of mouth-watering dishes by celebrity chefs. A lengthy spell on rice and beans (not to mention Bushtucker) seemed ridiculous, even if I was hoping to lose some weight. But, as my mother once said to President Bush during the run-up to Operation Desert Storm, 'This is no time to go wobbly.' So I signed up.

I soon discovered that in the world of reality TV the level of confidentiality can rival the Official Secrets Act. Rumours were rife about the identity of my fellow jungle mates, but any attempts I made to find out were met with stonewalling. And there was so much to do, starting with a grilling from the show's psychiatrist who asked a barrage of questions designed – I am sure – to ascertain my mental stability (or lack of it) before I was allowed to participate. I obliged, but remained a bit perplexed, they seemed to think that I would be a threat to the fragile balance of the Australian rainforest!

Was I nervous? I was asked.

'I don't bother worrying about anything until I've seen it,' I replied. Trying to sound invincible and Thatch-like. I added, 'If I don't want to do something, I won't. But that's unlikely.'

Then the wardrobe team arrived at my flat, with a vast amount of jungle gear. The first items were a rain jacket and snug sleeveless fleece, which had me reaching for my copy of *The Rough Guide to Australia* to check the rainfall and temperatures of the New South Wales/Queensland border. To my great amusement they made considerable efforts to ensure I'd look presentable for the duration of my stay. They proffered pairs of ski-resort-thickness scarlet socks; durable, heavy leather bush boots, khaki shirts, safari-style shorts, and some red camouflage trousers. I slipped these last on. 'Would you like them turned up?' someone asked. I couldn't believe it. The whole lot would, I was sure, be filthy within days so why were they offering me a tailored fit?

'No, thanks, I like my trouser bottoms scraping the ground,' I declared. Anyway, I wanted the surplus material to stuff into my boots, in order to minimise the chance of any reptiles, creepy-crawlies or furry friends making themselves comfortable.

I was also given one of Australia's famous Akubra bushman's hats. I saw mine as a friend of many guises, whether hiding messy hair or, with the brim pulled down, allowing me a sneaky forty winks. My next task was to film my contribution to the title sequence. I opted for an over-the-top look on the basis there was nothing to lose. I chose a full-length red leather coat I'd seen in Buenos Aires during my Falklands trip and fallen in love with. I wanted a matching scarlet bowler, but all I could get at the last minute in the market behind Waterloo Station was a jaunty red-felt one. It had to do.

Summoned to the set, I discovered a gleaming white stretch limo surrounded by fake palm trees.

I was mildly amused to see that the limo's number plate was U GO 2 WED. After all, many a celebrity had done quite well in the marriage stakes. Peter Andre and Katie Price had recently staged a very high-profile, very pink, wedding. Phil Tufnell, former Test cricketer and winner of the second series, had gone on to marry his girlfriend. Maybe the show fancied itself as a dating agency.

The director told me to emerge from the rear of the limo and walk towards the camera, brushing aside any palm fronds along the way. That didn't seem too arduous. 'The celeb before took thirty takes!' one of the crew confided.

Having done my bit, I was told to leave the set so that I didn't accidentally bump into any of my fellow contestants – bringing back memories of Mum's concerns on accepting the role of PM from the Queen. My driver reversed his car onto the film lot and I hopped in.

Suddenly a message crackled through on the radio: 'Paparazzi outside.'

'Could you lie on the back seat, please?' one of the crew asked. It was essential that my identity not be discovered until the show began. As I made myself horizontal, the farcical nature of my predicament struck me. I felt like stolen goods being moved around surreptitiously. It seemed very ironic that, having signed up for a show where we would be under surveillance around the clock, here I was in the middle of London wondering whether I would be allowed to sit up by the time we reached Marble Arch.

My last few days in London reminded me of how fidgety my mother used to get in the weeks between calling a general election and polling day itself. There were a few last-minute, alcohol-fuelled farewell lunches before it was time to say goodbye to Mum, who never really took in what I was doing. I just told her I was off on another one of my Australian jaunts, but decided not to try to explain about the show, which she would never watch anyway. Mark came to lend his support and, before I left, he gave me an expensive multi-purpose knife for the jungle. Unfortunately, the powers-that-be decreed that such a useful item wouldn't be allowed, but it was a much appreciated gesture.

There was just time to collect my one luxury item, a collapsible candy-striped chair, before my flight. I had decided that, instead of heading straight for Brisbane and coping with the jetlag and heat all at once, I would have a stopover at Hua Hin, a quiet beach resort in Thailand. As I relaxed alone, I psyched myself up for the challenges ahead. I was convinced that I would be voted to do the first Bushtucker Trial, as some viewers, still angry at my mother and her policies, might see that as a good way of getting back at her.

Preparation seemed to be the key and by that I didn't mean munching my way through a selection of ingredients *before* they were tossed into the stir fry at the nearest Thai night market. No, I wanted to take a bit of time to gain some perspective and, hopefully, convince myself that whatever I was chomping, it could be worse. My mother had always said, 'Time spent in reconnaissance is seldom wasted,' so I sat on my terrace one evening, cold beer in hand, with a notebook and pen on my lap and decided to prepare my strategy.

I had a copy of *The Lonely Planet Guide to Cambodia* with me because I was planning to visit the Angkor Wat temples there after the show. On the page about a place called Skuon, my attention

was drawn to a passage about its claim to fame. 'Skuon is affection-
ately known as 'Spiderville' because the locals eat eight-legged
furry friends for breakfast, lunch and dinner . . . the creatures –
decidedly dead – are [fried and] piled high on platters . . . They are
best treated like a crab and eaten by cracking the body open and
pulling the legs off one by one, bringing the juiciest flesh out with
them . . . Watch for the abdomen, which seems to be filled with
some pretty nasty tasting brown sludge, which could be anything
from eggs to excrement . . .'

How monstrously disgusting. I reached into my minibar for
another frosty Chang Thai beer, feeling fairly confident that, with
the spiders in mind, I could face most things a bush deli might put
on the menu. The *Rough Guide* gave me some clues under its
'Infamous Australian Foods' section: 'Witchetty Grubs – about the
size of your little finger, [they] are dug from the roots of the mulga
trees and are a well-known Australian delicacy. Eating the plump,
fawn-coloured caterpillars live takes some nerve, so try giving them
a brief roasting in embers. They're very tasty either way –
reminiscent of peanut butter.' Well, I was going to have to petition
Ant and Dec to pass my ration over a barbie, or else brief my taste
buds that the flavour sensation was the first cousin to a peanut
butter and jelly sandwich. Needless to say, by now my appetite for
dinner had evaporated.

Another concern was that the professional actors and
performers likely to be among my fellow celebrities would be far
better equipped than I to improvise, recall a witty gag penned for

them, or deliver a punchline with knock-out success. They would simply regard their run in the jungle as another role to be played out in front of a TV audience. With no RADA training and zero acting ability, what you see with me really is what you get. I worried about whether I would be able to conjure up something insightful or amusing to say when twenty thousand cockroaches were advancing up my inner thighs. Or would blind panic paralyse me?

Following my mother's example, I decided to write myself some preparatory notes about what to do when faced with a difficult task: 'Eating: Get it down and remark in the manner of an esteemed restaurant critic, "This would be better with ketchup," or make a subtle comment on the seasoning. Request the wine list, which could also buy time if the occasion demanded.

'Creatures: Make friends, but if they become too affectionate, suggest in your best dating-agency tone that they try one of their own kind.'

I also mugged up on Australia, and bought a CD of Aussie music, which I played over and over again. Heaven knows what the folks in the next room thought about me singing along tunelessly to 'Waltzing Matilda' or 'The Pub with No Beer'. My logic was that chanting a few native lyrics while shifting firewood, boiling the billy, and performing other chores might break up the monotony. Better still, while having to endure something prolonged and ghastly, singing might take my mind off it.

Leaving Thailand reluctantly, I flew down to Brisbane reading

Bill Bryson's book *Down Under* through the night – still making notes. I was only at page nineteen when I began to feel that perhaps this wasn't for those of a nervous disposition. 'Of the world's ten most poisonous snakes, all are Australian. Five of its creatures – the funnel-web spider, box jellyfish, blue-ringed octopus, paralysis tick and stonefish – are the most lethal of their type in the world. This is a country where even the fluffiest of caterpillars can lay you out with a toxic nip, where seashells will not just sting you but actually sometimes go for you . . .' I reached for the overhead light. Surely even the sadistic producers of this epic would appreciate that it's not good telly to kill off the contestants?

When I stepped off the plane, the journalists were waiting. 'How will you cope with the bugs?' they wanted to know.

'I'll give it a go.'

'Who do you think will win?'

'One of the young TV stars,' I predicted, and I meant it.

'Don't you think "Thatcher, Queen of the Jungle" has a nice ring to it?' one said. I grinned.

In the baggage hall I couldn't help but notice the huge roulette wheel on top of the carousel, which seemed to me to underline the gamble I was taking.

Booked into a suite at the Marriot Hotel in Surfer's Paradise under the alias of 'Loni Anderson' – she's an American actress and one-time wife of Burt Reynolds! – I caught up with texts and e-mails. Friends in London fed me the breaking news about my jungle dorm mates, with reassuring comments that the tabloids were being much worse to the soap stars than to me. Then the telephone rang and I learned that the *Daily Mirror*, hardly a Thatcher supporter over the decades, had a leader that day entitled, 'Vote Thatch'. Not Mum, but me. I couldn't believe it! I was on the radar already. My confidence went up and I suppose I had an inkling of how my ma must have felt when the opinion polls had given her a decent lead at the beginning of an election campaign. I was going to need to dig deep for my genes, remembering all that I'd learned from being on the inside of a political family, looking out. What I needed was a good dose of the Aussie 'Just fucking do it' attitude. I also hoped to discover a few new Thatcher qualities and hidden dimensions.

My last supper was a selection of oysters, some lovely wine and it was then I started to worry.

Having parachuted or trekked our way into the jungle (I had to skydive in and promptly threw up), I and my fellow campers – soap actors Sid Owen, Elaine Lordan and Sheree Murphy, singer Jimmy Osmond, comedians Tommy Cannon and Bobby Ball, wine buff Jilly Goolden, television presenter David Dickinson, singers Jenny Frost and Antony Costa, and *Neighbours* actress Kimberley Davies – soon settled down to a daily routine.

As with most group excursions, life in camp was limited and predictable in such a small, confined world. There were chores of course, such as lugging armfuls of firewood up to the camp:

the fire had to be kept going, day and night to ward off critters. Water pots had to be filled from the river and then the contents boiled before being filtered through the porous lining of Jimmy Osmond's swimming shorts, cleverly improvised for the task.

We got to know quite a lot about one another rather in the course of fireside conversations. As a showbiz groupie, I was intrigued to hear Jimmy's tales of the heyday of the Osmonds, when he and his brothers had to be smuggled into hotels through kitchens or other bizarre entry points to avoid the crowds of fans outside. Jimmy let slip that he had spoken to Elvis Presley on the telephone a number of times and that the Osmonds had even been on stage with the King a few times. These were mesmerising reminiscences for a star-struck kid whose upbringing, by comparison, had been in mere politics.

Wanting to remember every detail of camp life, I kept a diary, written on the back of any scraps of paper which came my way, usually the supper menus – which were a far cry from those I'd kept from dinners at Number Ten or the White House. In the jungle, my meals comprised kangaroo, wallaby and an assortment of bush veggies I'd never heard of, rather than paupiettes of salmon or some fabulous beef dish. In the margins I scribbled notes using fresh charcoal (often still warm) from the campfire. Jimmy Osmond had a particularly good production line in the stuff.

Every day brought a new Bushtucker Trial and, predictably, I was chosen for quite a few of them, including the first, which involved 'driving' a scarlet mini-car along a high-wire over a ravine with a hundred-foot drop, to collect stars. Sadly, I lost my balance and my vehicle plummeted to the bottom of the ravine, landing as a pile of bent metal. That had been one of the hairiest moments.

The worst trial, by far, was having to do the one thing I had tried to psyche myself up for: eating live creatures. I shared the hideous task with gourmet Jilly Goolden. We sat opposite each other at a table and took turns to be presented with one creepy-crawlie after another, lurking beneath wooden domes that were lifted off as if we were dining at some silver service gentleman's club. Keeping the fried spiders of Skuon and the sea slugs of Beijing constantly in my mind, I managed to munch my way through cheese fruit (more aptly known as 'vomit fruit'), describing it as 'quite spicy, quite filling, rather bitter'. Jilly opted for the green ants, and then it was on to the grasshoppers, to whom I apologised before biting off their heads. Jilly balked at the cockroach but, after a quick pep talk from yours truly, bravely tucked in.

Next, I tackled a witchetty grub, whose inner mucus dripped down my chin disgustingly. That was a tough one and I must admit to almost returning it in a projectile fashion to the plate, but gave myself a good talking to along the lines of 'Get on with it – the troops want some dinner.' Buying time as I instructed my stomach not to upchuck, I asked Ant and Dec if one of the sheets of paper they were holding wasn't the wine list.

The next course consisted of a fish eye for me, which was so tough it must have been wearing a contact lens, while Jilly passed on the rat's tail. Dessert was perhaps the yuckiest of all – kangaroo's testicle for me, which was squelchy and horrid, and a kangaroo penis for Jilly, which was so chewy it had to be cut in half. After our sterling efforts, we won eight out of nine possible stars and returned to camp triumphant and still picking unspeakable body parts from our teeth.

Ant and Dec said later that my eating trial was done in the quickest time ever. 'Before we could say "Carol, the next one is witchetty grubs," it was in your gob!' I pointed out that the grub was still wriggling after I'd taken a bite out of it and that I'd rather admired it for that. But I couldn't bear the expression on the faces of its mates – in case I fancied seconds.

When I wasn't voted for a Bushtucker Trial, there was a huge feeling of relief and then sympathy for the person who had been picked. There was still plenty to do, though: cooking, cleaning, washing, preening, cleaning out the loos. Caught on camera in the middle of the night having a quick pee (rather than traipse through the dark to the loos), I was reprimanded by the TV bosses and more than a little embarrassed to have been caught, but one of the beauties of middle-age is that nothing much fazes me any more and I soon forgot about it.

Our other daily task was the hunt for the Treasure Chest, which usually involved a pair of us setting out from camp armed with a map to locate the chest and its key and then jump through hoops (or worse) to release it from its perch in a towering gum tree or other immoveable obstacle. My first experience of chest-hunting was with Tony Costa, and we had to use a rusty handsaw with blunt teeth to free it from its shackles. Another chest expedition turned into an overnight adventure, when Sid Owen and I found ourselves trapeze-walking over a primitive rope bridge, stretched across a ravine, to a giant spider's web. The chest and key retrieved, our rope bridge snapped behind us, an event we weren't sure was meant to happen.

Unknown to me, and taking the mickey out of my inability to say my Rs, Ant told the viewers, 'Cawol bwoke the wope bwidge and you know what that means . . .' Dec continued, 'Stwanded.' Later, they claimed that when I thanked the producers for extra rations of eggs, sausages and beans (not to mention the beer and wine) in the mini-camp they'd set up for Sid and me overnight, I'd described it as a 'tweat and a twiumph'. What I'd actually said, on seeing a flushing loo and proper camp beds, was, 'We've been upgraded, mate. This will have Michelin stars next.'

Food, or rather the lack of, became a serious issue, especially for those who had no weight to lose. I felt more pressure than ever to go for it by the time of my third Bushtucker Trial, entitled Noah's Ark. There were only five of us left by then – Sheree, Sid, Bobby, Jimmy and me. Jimmy was gracious enough to declare that, 'If anyone can do it, it's you.' With Noah's Ark conjuring up all sorts of two-by-two images of large beasts, I said, 'I'm no lion tamer.' In the end, I had to don a latex wetsuit and swim across a critter-infested lake wearing a large Perspex 'Ark' on my head to collect the coveted yellow stars, along with the occupants of the boxes in which the stars lay. I wasn't worried about the swimming, because at home several times a week I used to swim a mile in a local pool. But when the show's animal expert, Bob McCarron, arrived to brief me on the identity and nature of my hitchhikers, my adrenalin began to flow.

'All these creatures are capable of biting/scratching/hanging onto you,' he warned. 'We do have a couple of species of snake: very fast-moving tree snakes and constrictors. None is poisonous but they can bite. The poisonous animals are the cane toads [which] excrete venom from their side glands. Try not to get it on your lips. If you do, try not to lick your lips; leave it there and we can wipe it off afterwards.'

He didn't warn me about the rhinoceros beetles, the cockroaches and the rats that would also be scurrying around my head in the Ark. I could only imagine what sort of combat might be happening between them all in the vicinity of my ears as I revved up my breaststroke and powered across the lake. 'Speed up, Thatch!' I encouraged myself out loud.

On the bank, Ant announced, 'Dressed from head to toe in a black wetsuit, she looks like something out of a Bond film.'

Dec hammed up the Bond theme. 'Her name is Thatch – C. Thatch, licensed to . . .'

Having been such a fan of the movies as a teenager, thirty years

283

later in a murky Australian lake I was a Bond Girl, even if it was only for a few minutes.

When a rat started nibbling my cheek, I yelled, 'Stop kissing me. I prefer something attached to two legs, not four.' At their departure box, I maintained the bossy approach. 'This is where you disembark,' I said, dipping them and the yellow star in. Next were the promised cane toads, one of which completed the voyage clinging to the top of my head. 'Upper Class?' I enquired. As venomous passengers go they were well behaved and probably as glad as I was when they were released at their destination. Two more stars to go and then the last 'mystery box', which was full of water spiders. No trouble and I had five stars – which meant five full meals for us all.

'Is that it?' I asked Ant and Dec on the bank. 'Can I do it again?' I had visions of nabbing a gooey dessert or something else for dinner. Sadly, the answer was no.

After a group trial called Slippery Slope, which was basically an adult Waterworld in which we had to slide down a muddy slope and then crawl up it inelegantly with our stars, and a fancy-dress promenade in which I was, thankfully, not asked to model on the catwalk but to be the compere, there were just three of us left – Sid, Sheree, and me. I couldn't believe I had made it this far. I had fully expected to be among the first evicted – and three weeks later here I was, in the running for the title Queen of the Jungle.

During the last few days I had been asked a number of times in the Bush Telegraph (an interview booth on the campsite) why people were apparently voting for me. Researching my 1983 book *Diary of an Election*, I had asked my mother, 'What, as Britain's first woman Prime Minister, have you brought to the job?

Her reply taught me a valuable lesson. 'I'm not the person to answer that question,' she said. Citing her example, I told them I had no idea why people were voting for me. It was their choice, not mine. But what I did know was that I was grateful for their support.

After sixteen days of being hermetically sealed off and totally isolated – our only horizons the camp boundaries – my thoughts turned to the future. I had planned this amazing backpacking trip immediately after the show. I was heading for the ruins of Sukhothai in Northern Thailand, then on to Luang Prabang on the Mekong river. I had been fascinated by rivers ever since being spellbound as a child by the eddies, flows and tides, barges and tourist boats on the Thames viewed from the terrace of the House of Commons. In Luang Prabang I planned to take a boat up the Mekong to the Pak Ou Buddha Caves, which housed hundreds and hundreds of Buddha images. Then on to Angkor Wat in Cambodia and the Ta Prohm Khmer temple complex, almost lost in the jungle, where thousand-year-old banyan trees with roots the diameter of stone columns grip the crumbling masonry of the temple walls and spires. Finally, to Saigon for Christmas.

Gazing into the campfire, lost in my itinerary, I had a nagging thought: suppose, as can occasionally happen to rank outsiders, I won? Would my Asian jaunt have to be canned in order to fulfil my winner's responsibilities? I dismissed it from my mind. How could I possibly win, when I was so much the odd one out compared with beautiful Sheree and her legion of *Emmerdale* followers and Liverpool football fans, and Sid with his millions of *Eastenders* fans and girls enamoured of his charm and good looks? In politics, though, it is misguided to make plans or predictions. I had seen enough of the tension and hope involved in waiting for results while votes were counted. It was my turn to be patient now that for the first time in my life it was my name on the ballot paper.

The final morning arrived and with it the announcement that there were three Bushtucker Trials – one for each of us – entitled, Uncover, Discover and Undercover. I opted for Uncover, after naughtily suggesting that we didn't actually have to succeed as we could pig out in our luxury hotel. Not the point at all, Thatch! As I set off for my fifth and last trial, I was slightly nervous, as I didn't want to mess up at this stage. I arrived at the designated trial spot to hear Ant and Dec telling viewers, 'Carol Thatcher and Snake Strike. It was a terrifying prospect, but after lengthy discussions and numerous safety checks, the snakes finally agreed to take part.'

In the briefing with Bob McCarron before we went into the jungle, I had expressed the view that, of all the trials I might have to face, it was snakes I feared the most. Now here I was, peering into a huge glass chamber with portholes in the sides and at least twenty snakes of various sizes writhing around in the bottom or dangling from branches. Ant and Dec explained that I had to retrieve five numbered stars in order from the pit via the portholes and pass them round to a postbox in one side of the chamber. I could drop but not throw the stars.

'Dr Bob' gave me some final tips on snake etiquette. He told me to adopt a 'never mind them' attitude. That was unlikely enough, but I was really alarmed by the next bit of advice: what to do when one bit me. 'Don't pull your hand away because snake teeth are quite sharp and will drag along your skin. Leave your arm in there and one of us will help.' He helpfully confirmed that some snakes have up to sixty teeth. Yes, sixty.

I had three minutes: my glasses were misting up and sweat was running down my back. I had researched lots of snakes in an internet café during my Thailand stopover. 'Not as dangerous as they make you believe,' said the guidebook. I picked the first star out of a cavity in a log. Luckily the nearest snake slithered off, and I passed the star round, cautiously poking my arms in and out of portholes, until it was safely deposited in the postbox. The second star had to be accessed via a porthole covered in clingfilm, which I had to punch through to reach the residents – spiders – and release a key which fell into the snake chamber. I blurted a well-mannered, 'Excuse me, folks,' to them and got on with it. Another star. The next was in a first-aid box on the floor of the chamber, which I opened to spot the star hiding beneath a pile of small snakes. My instinct was to withdraw my hand but advice from a friend in London flashed through my mind: 'Just go for it.'

Creatures take time to twig that you are there.' Extremely carefully and expecting any minute the stinging sensation of an irritated snake biting me, I used my finger and thumb and got it. I was running out of time and there were still some baby crocs to contend with – which worried me far less than the snakes. I managed, after a bit of a panic, to post the last star in the postbox with a mere two seconds to go. The relief! 'Victoire, Thatch!' I crowed. 'Anacondas, you lost!' A ranger subsequently told me that I was very lucky not to have been bitten.

I made my way back to camp and told Sid and Sheree the good news. Sheree went on to give a heroine's performance eating ghastly critters, and Sid gritted his teeth and closed his mouth to be buried underground with water and a sizeable number of rats. A bottle of French champagne was delivered, the sun shone, our last dinner was delicious, and Sid said it all: 'We've done it. We've lasted. We're relieved and we can't wait to get out.'

The following morning, I cherished every second of lying in my sleeping bag gazing up at the hundred-foot-high gum trees as the sun glinted through them. I thought back over camp life. My early fears that I would be mercilessly beaten up for being Maggie's daughter had never materialised. True, in a quiz I should have known that Finland was in the Euro zone, and identified the country's currency correctly. Even more embarrassing was being asked to attribute the quote, 'Power is like being a lady: if you have to tell people you've got it, you haven't.' I hadn't a clue. The correct answer was: Margaret Thatcher.

Whatever the day brought, I had done way better than I ever had dared hope. Life-changing? No. Life-enhancing? Certainly, even if it would inevitably fade into perspective as just two-and-a-bit weeks camped in a rainforest. As I got up and headed for our rock pool for one last wash, it dawned on me that I was in the final three. In my mind, against all the odds. Win, lose or draw, it didn't matter.

But I was wrong. When I won, it certainly did matter.

Chapter Fifteen

COMING UP FOR AIR

Being crowned Queen of the Jungle was unbelievably exciting, and it was a revelation a minute. Having been hermetically sealed in a jungle capsule, I was astonished to be told by the TV executives that 12 million people had watched the final night, 1.5 million votes had been cast – and I got 1 million of them.

My mother had always taught me to be gracious and grateful to supporters, and at that moment, I made up my mind about something. That when I got out, however many times I heard the same jokes about bush-tucker trials and camp life, that I would always make an effort to be the jolly and thankful person people had got to know on the show. They might be strangers, but they had supported me and now it seemed that lots of them had actually spent money voting for me.

While I was relaxing in my luxury hotel suite afterwards, my mobile phone glowed with euphoric text messages from friends back home. Logging on to a computer, I found my inbox bursting with messages and invitations – my first inkling of what was to come.

One of the first e-mails I opened was from my brother, an infrequent correspondent. In the header he'd simply typed, *'Wow'* and then went on:

Brilliant, Brilliant, Brilliant. You are a hero over here and the press have gone mad. Amazing stuff. Every time I get in a cab all the cabbies ask after you and say how great you have been – which you have . . . Words not my strong suit but I want you to know that you had the balls to take it on against all advice (thankfully not mine) and you beat the lot of them. Bloody marvellous. Congrats, salaams and everything else . . . The headlines are 'Iron Lady II'. Brilliant . . . proud to be your brother. Fondest love, Mark.

Now I was truly overwhelmed.

Then there were the many messages from the friends who'd suggested it would be better not to touch the programme with a barge pole. The sentiment was either 'humble pie' or 'eating our words' but it didn't matter; all were loaded with warm and genuine congratulations. It didn't take long for me to get the picture back home, particularly when friends told me I'd made the front cover of just about every newspaper and a researcher from Radio 4's *Today* programme rang for an interview. (I got the impression that covering *I'm a Celeb* wasn't really their thing.) A correspondent later wrote to thank me for saying kangaroo testicles 'not once but at least twice, on the *Today* programme'.

Back in London life was giddier than I ever could have imagined: loads of queries from complete strangers about eating kangaroo bollocks and, of course, the notorious Pee-gate.

I wore a fixed and beaming toothpaste-ad-like grin whenever I was treated to more jokes on these two items. I also developed a useful veneer of unembarrassability.

Nothing, however, prepared me for the public outpouring of goodwill. For a short while I couldn't walk down the street without being stopped. I had to pinch myself that this was really happening to me after years of seeing it happen to my mother.

One day, on the way back from my regular swim, a well-dressed commuter stopped, stared, and said, 'Carol?' He told me his children would never forgive him if he failed to get my autograph. With that he whipped out a blank sheet of A4 from his briefcase, produced a pen and waited for me to complete the not very arduous task of dashing off another 'Best Wishes from The Queen of the Jungle.'

More often than not, I was asked to pose in front of mobile phones on some street corner while out shopping. Of course, I willingly obliged. There's no doubt that being an 'in' person, if only for a short while, was a tremendous boost to morale and I bubbled along on a crescendo. The first television appearance I made on my return was on GMTV. As I sat in my dressing room texting friends I knew to be early risers, there was a knock on the door. Assuming it was my cue to go to the studio, I leaped up to open it, and found fellow guest Tony Blair standing there clutching a mug of coffee.

'Prime Minister!' I gulped in amazement.

'Congratulations,' he said, explaining that his kids had been glued to the show. I was enormously chuffed.

Only ten days out of the jungle, I was asked to appear on *Ant & Dec's Saturday Night Takeaway* Christmas Special, and I accepted – I assumed the format would be along the lines of Yuletide-tucker Trial: moi to slide down a length of (very) reinforced tinsel and participate in a prank like a snowball or mince-pie fight.

Then the costume department phoned. 'Don't worry, Carol, because your bloomers will be embroidered with Merry Christmas on them, in case you come off.'

Eh? Come off what? Alarm bells began to jangle.

It turned out that, rather than some gentle chat with Ant and Dec, my stunt consisted of hopping into a Santa mini-dress worn with tarty, sparkly silver shoes and baggy bloomers straight out of a panto. To top it off, the make-up team planted on my head a wig of golden plaits seemingly borrowed from a damsel in an Edam cheese commercial.

I was mounted on an inflatable Rudolph the red-nosed reindeer, and when a button was pressed he went into bucking-bronco mode. I was catapulted off, which must have looked highly inelegant; still, a good third of the audience should have got to read the festive message on my bloomers. I then grabbed a parcel and chucked it in the direction of Ant & Dec.

The starstruck bit was shaking hands with Robbie Williams during his gala rendition of 'White Christmas'.

Once you become a well-known face on television, members of the public regard you as alternative entertainment. Flying to Dublin to appear on *The Late Late Show*, I had to catch an early flight. I wasn't feeling too much like a Jungle Queen so I headed to the coffee shop, hoping a large cappuccino would revive me. En route, I was spotted by a group of children on a day trip to Lapland. For half an hour, I signed autographs, answered questions, posed for photos with the kids for their mums and dads using mobile phones. I even saw one dad buying a disposable camera so his child could be snapped with me.

A few weeks later at Heathrow, I was trundling down the ramp to the baggage carousel, jet-lagged and bleary-eyed after an overnight flight, when I heard the sound of running feet behind me. Not wanting to get in anyone's way, I moved to one side so they could pass, only to find two fellow passengers bang in front of me. 'It *is* you!' they cried excitedly. 'We weren't sure. Could we have your autograph?' More mobile phone moments followed, although I'm sure I wasn't looking my best. Another morning I was walking along the South Bank, close to where I live, past a new restaurant which was preparing to open. There was a menu outside so I stopped to see what was on it. As I perused the options, a workman on a ladder overhead shouted down, 'Better than you got in the jungle, Thatch!'

What gave me so much pleasure was having been part of a series which had been such a success with the viewers that they wanted to talk to me about it. For a few days I almost kidded myself that I had made it on to the celebrity plateau where you're known by only one name – in my case, Thatch.

So, given my previous life as merely the prime minister's daughter, I had to ponder what the difference was between second-hand and first-hand fame. Well, now the questions about the jungle came first. One weekend I went up to Hull to support Tommy Cannon and Bobby Ball, who were in the pantomime *Dick Whittington*. I was really looking forward to meeting up again with these two super chaps and reminiscing with them about jungle life. I spent most of the rail journey signing autographs for the train staff. Then, when I got there, those two funny men got me up on stage to take a bow at the end, and after the performance I stood alongside them signing autographs outside the stage door. It was heady stuff.

One of the most ironic moments in the days that followed my win was when I went to see Elton John's musical based on the film *Billy Elliot* with some friends. In the production, my mother is portrayed as the arch baddy, because much of the plot is set in County Durham during the national miners' strike of 1984–85 when Arthur Scargill, president of the National Union of Mineworkers, called a strike against the policy of pit closures introduced by the National Coal Board. In one scene, an image of my mother's face appears and the actors all wear Union Flag boxer shorts and sing 'Merry Christmas, Maggie Thatcher'. The lyrics include the chorus: *'Merry Christmas Maggie Thatcher, May God's love be with you. We all sing together in one breath, Merry Christmas Maggie Thatcher, We all celebrate today, 'Cos it's one day closer to your death.'*

Fortunately, the anti-Thatcher sentiment didn't stop members of the audience asking the daughter of the baddy for her autograph during the intermission. I had to giggle. One punter even took my glass of white wine out of my hand and replaced it with a glass of champagne because she said I 'deserved it'.

Bags of letters arrived at my London home, many simply addressed to 'Carol Thatcher, Queen of the Jungle, I'm a Celebrity Get Me Out of Here, England.' I heard from friends and strangers, people I hadn't seen since my schooldays, and women who claimed I was an inspiration to the over-fifties. Others were simply pleased at my triumph and requested something I'd never been asked for before – even as the daughter of Britain's first woman prime minister – signed photographs. My testicle-eating feat inspired special admiration, and was something that was to haunt me for years to come.

One seventy-eight-year-old retired nurse and staunch Labour supporter even suggested that, if I ever ran for political office, she'd change her allegiance and vote for me. Several had bet on me winning, and one punter was especially pleased as she had put £3 on me when I was ranked 8:1. Strangely, those had been the odds against my mother in her first leadership contest.

Deciding to take my planned trip to Asia at last, and escape the madness of the previous few weeks, I went to Heathrow straight after appearing on my usual slot reviewing the newspapers on Andrew Marr's BBC Sunday morning show. I was flying economy with Thai Airways and was immediately offered a free upgrade. On board, I texted a friend that I thought that was remarkably generous, as the staff might have got the impression that I would have preferred to jump from the plane and skydive into Bangkok.

On Christmas morning I took the lift up to the hotel's rooftop swimming pool for a dip. The doors opened on another floor first and I came face to face with Santa Claus in full regalia, a sack of presents over his shoulder and in ho-ho-ho bell-ringing mode. 'Do you have any children?' he asked reaching into his sack.

'No,' I replied, with a broad smile.

Truth was, I didn't need any. I didn't need anything. After years of living in my mother's shadow, I felt that I had finally found my niche after the most exhilarating few weeks of my life. It was Christmas Day. A new, exciting year loomed, full of post-jungle challenges, some of which would be a surprise.

*

Back home again in London, I soon discovered that, once you're a winner yourself, you are suddenly (and slightly incongruously) in demand to dish out awards to other victors. It was an interesting process to master.

First you have to get yourself onto the stage – probably in the ballroom of one of the hotels along Park Lane – without either tripping up or falling down the steps. An organiser will have handed you an envelope. 'And the nominees,' you trumpet, 'are . . .' (a strident voice inherited from my ma came in useful on the occasions when the mike was on the blink). More than once I crossed my fingers that I wouldn't mispronounce household names I'd never have heard of because chart-topping girl and boy bands are not my specialist subject. Then it's a question of ripping open the envelope and announcing the winner. After that, scarper back to the bar!

One of my invitations was to present one of the prizes at the Comedy Awards, hosted by Jonathan Ross. He joked that I couldn't say my Rs, which was a bit cheeky, since neither can he. Then there was a makeover and modelling session for a glossy magazine, so I got hair extensions and enjoyed the glamorous look for a while.

Another rather amusing ceremony was the Fifi Awards, top-notch prizes for fine fragrances. Thoughtfully, the organisers handed the awards presenters pronunciation guidelines – just in case we'd sat next to the window in French lessons.

Also memorable was the Fido Awards, which gives prizes for dogs in films. My category was won by the corgis in that terrific film *The Queen*, for which Dame Helen Mirren picked up so many accolades. Megan, one of the corgis, was trotted on and I handed the award to her owner – rather at arm's length, I have to confess, as I suddenly recalled my dad's warnings about corgis' tantrums from his acquaintance with them at Balmoral.

Unembarrassability came in handy when I was a guest presenter on a BBC television show *City Hospital*. It was filmed at St Thomas' and Guy's Hospitals and went out in the mornings. In the afternoon, production staff would call presenters to chat through the issues, patients and/or doctors they would be covering the following day.

'Carol, tomorrow morning you're at Guy's,' my briefing started. Then came the bombshell: 'How will you be in the erectile dysfunction clinic?'

'*Whattt?!!?* I mean … I'll just be asking the questions, not actually *demonstrating* anything, won't I?' I quavered, panic rising to high.

I was thrilled to be asked to be the 2006 face of British Sausage Week. Sausages and mash is one of my favourite dishes and Borough Market, which I can walk to along the River Thames in about ten minutes, has numerous outlets selling the best.

After a launch and a photocall on my roof terrace overlooking St Paul's, the itinerary had a small group of us heading up and down the country in search of the best sausage sarnie. The road show rolled through Newcastle, Leeds, Manchester, Nottingham and Birmingham, and wrapped in Bristol. The competitors were full of imagination, and highly foodie combinations such as 'Back from Bonfire Night' bangers were placed before the judges. This particular one was mega: oven-baked traditional chunky pork sausages with pumpkin wedges, sweetcorn chunks and large field mushrooms sprinkled with rosemary and drizzled with maple syrup, and stuffed into big round focaccia . . .

Lighter fare came in the shape of dinky mini hot dogs for dunking, which were chipolatas grilled and served in mini pittas with a selection of dips. I thought the Ultimate Brunch Breakfast Sarnie (pan-cooked sausages cooked with sliced cooked potatoes, tomato wedges, mushrooms and fried egg served as a wedge on a large slice of toasted white bread) would guarantee to erase the most vicious of hangovers.

At one venue in Bristol, a young Indian waiter told me that when the Commonwealth Heads of Government Meeting was held in India, his village had been so excited at the prospect of my mother's motorcade passing by that the road had been widened and the houses painted, and crowds lined the route waiting to cheer.

Alas, my mother went by helicopter.

I could have cried I felt so awful. Posing with him for a photo didn't seem anything like adequate compensation. I contemplated covering Mum's dining-room table a metre deep with photos of her to sign with a 'Sorry!' and mailing them all off.

The *Daily Mail* invited me to take part in a more de luxe version of the jungle than the *I'm a Celeb* set-up, and I flew off to Guatemala, where Francis Ford Coppola, the Oscar-winning director of *The Godfather* and other brilliant films, owns three extremely comfortable lodges awash with creature comforts.

Up at La Lancha, on the shores of glinting Lake Petén in northern Guatemala, not far from the awesome Mayan ruins at Tikal, I was woken very early by the resonant bark of howler monkeys. As a sundowner, I enjoyed a glass of house chardonnay from a Californian winery Coppola owns in Napa Valley, along with filmstars Robert DeNiro and Robin Williams. This was the red-carpet jungle, all right!

One of the souvenirs my mother had collected on her travels, and which in our hasty move out of Number Ten had turned up in one of my boxes, was a coconut painted with a gay and appealingly gaudy sunset scene. It was from Belize, where I went to another Coppola property, Blancaneaux Lodge in the forests of Mountain Pine Ridge. Connoisseurs of movie paraphernalia enjoyed the fan in the bar – the very same one which had stirred the humid air above Martin Sheen's head in the opening sequence of *Apocalypse Now*.

There was one brief minus moment. I have never been terribly keen on flying in small planes or helicopters in tropical conditions. Somehow a combination of the heat and the bumping around caused by the thermals makes me feel rather nauseous.

Just before I took off from a jungle airstrip, the pretty girl pilot in perfectly pressed white uniform asked me how I was in small planes. 'OK,' I ventured. We took off and I concentrated on admiring the lush scenery. 'I don't want you to be alarmed,' she said reaching across me, 'but I just need to close your door.' A slam and that was it. I looked down at the vast coffee plantation below and hoped that, had I dropped out of the unlocked door, my death certificate would have read 'Died grinding the coffee beans – and the bushes!'

Rather misguidedly, I agreed to do a tap-dancing routine for a TV competition. I took endless lessons in Covent Garden, and the girls in my chorus line were absolute gems. The poor choreographer twigged how useless I was when, after another rehearsal of my gorilla gyrations, she suggested I would find it easier with the music.

'No,' I wailed, 'that will only confuse me more.'

One of the judges, the American David Gest, who followed me into the jungle, was spot-on with his assessment of my performance. His verdict was that he'd seen more interesting bowel movements than my disastrous dancing efforts!

I was on the panel of *Question Time* the week the news broke that the then deputy prime minister, John Prescott, had been having an affair with his secretary.

A lady in the audience stood up and asked what she could have seen in Prezza. David Dimbleby nominated me to answer first. Oh, help! Did I ever think I would have to assess the fanciability (or lack of it) of Two Jags live on TV?

I did what my mother had always advised me to do: repeat the question slowly, because this gives the impression that you consider it thoughtful/interesting/intelligent, and buys you time to scramble an answer.

Post-jungle fame was full of one-offs. A Heathrow immigration officer once greeted me with the statement: 'You were the clue in a crossword puzzle I was doing and I couldn't remember your first name.' As if it was all my fault and I was responsible for her missing out on a £20 voucher to the races!

*

Now that my innings in the goldfish bowl is long over, I find I am just as inquisitive as everyone else on the outside peering in through the glass. Maybe more so, because I know what it was like to have that swim-on part for a while. When, as a young journalist I was sent to write a feature on The Lodge in Canberra – the Australian Prime Minister's residence, which was open to the public, I was delighted to make the gleeful discovery that his soup spoons on the dining room table didn't match. Yet, when it was our turn to be scrutinised whilst in Number Ten, I always went on the defensive when a guest observed that the net curtains were grubby.

How easy it is to change sides!

I admire those whose turn it is now: Chelsea Clinton and her enthusiasm and energy as she criss-crossed America, campaigning to have her mum elected as the first female president. Jenna Bush, whose grandfather had been president, and whose father still was when she chose to get married down on her father's Texas ranch, rather than go for a whopping White House extravaganza.

The bottom line of second-hand fame consists in not being strangled or intimidated – and remembering there's always someone ahead of you. However elevated you think you are, it's all about perspective.

On the topic of not being intimidated by others, I always quote the Ronald Reagan approach. When Gorbachev visited Washington, and President Reagan was waiting to greet him in the White House, a journalist asked whether he resented the Russian leader's tremendous popularity. The President replied that he didn't and added for good measure: 'Good Lord, I co-starred with Errol Flynn once.'

For me, the role of Daughter of has consisted of enjoying the privileges, surviving the knocks and relishing the challenge of stamping my personality on it.

BIBLIOGRAPHY

Campbell, John: *Margaret Thatcher, The Grocer's Daughter*, Pimlico, 2001

—— *Margaret Thatcher, Iron Lady*, Vintage, 2007

Clark, Alan: *Alan Clark Diaries*, Weidenfeld & Nicolson, 2000

McAlpine, Alistair: *Once a Jolly Bagman*, Phoenix, 1997

Major, Norma: *Chequers*, HarperCollins, 1996

Marr, Andrew: *A History of Modern Britain*, Macmillan, 2008

Millar, Ronald: *A View from the Wings*, Weidenfeld & Nicolson, 1993

Parris, Matthew: *Chance Witness: An Outsider's Life in Politics*, Viking, 2002

Sherrin, Ned: *A Small Thing Like an Earthquake*, Weidenfeld & Nicolson, 1993

Thatcher, Carol: *Diary of an Election*, Sidgwick & Jackson, 1983

—— *Below the Parapet*, HarperCollins, 1996

Thatcher, Margaret: *The Downing Street Years*, HarperCollins, 1993

—— *The Path to Power*, HarperCollins, 1995

PICTURE CREDITS

p 7, bottom © Getty Images

p 8, top © ITV/Rex Features

p 8, middle left © Nigel Wright/Rex Features

p 8, bottom © Tim Rooke/Rex Features